THE GREEK HISTORIANS

The Greeks invented history as a literary genre in the fifth century BC. The first historians owed much to Homer and adopted his vivid and direct style in narrating historical events, as well as adopting the themes of war and descriptions of foreign lands. Yet, despite the influence of Homer, the birth of history was basically a reaction against mythical accounts of the past. In contrast, the Greek historians of the fifth century wrote about contemporary or very recent events, where eye witnesses could be interviewed and facts cross-checked.

The Greek Historians follows the development of history from Herodotus, via Thucydides, Xenophon and the fragmentary historians who followed him, to Polybius at the end of the Hellenistic age. It introduces the individual writers and the subjects of their histories, yet it also outlines their attitudes to historiography and their criticisms of each other. Such themes as causation, historical truth and the uses and value of history are traced, as well as the growing constraints on free speech under Hellenistic monarchs and the Romans. Written in an accessible and captivating manner, with suggestions for further reading, this book serves as a lucid introduction to Greek historians and the writing of history.

T.J. Luce is Emeritus Professor of Classics at Princeton University. He has published widely on classical historiography and Roman history and is the author of *Livy: The Composition of his History* (1977).

THE GREEK
HISTORIANS

T.J. Luce

London and New York

First published 1997
by Routledge
11 New Fetter Lane, London EC4P 4EE

Simultaneously published in the USA and Canada
by Routledge
29 West 35th Street, New York, NY 10001

Typeset in Garamond by Routledge
Printed and bound in Great Britain by
T J Press (Padstow) Ltd, Padstow, Cornwall

British Library Cataloguing in Publication Data
A catalogue record for this book is available from the British Library

Library of Congress Cataloguing in Publication Data
Luce, T. James (Torry James), 1932–
The Greek historians / T.J. Luce.
Includes bibliographical references and index.
1. Greece–History–To 146 BC–Historiography. 2. History, Ancient–
Historiography. 3. Historiography–Greece–History. I. Title.
DF211.L83 1997
938–dc20
96–19960
CIP

ISBN 0–415–10592–7 (hbk)
ISBN 0–415–10593–5 (pbk)

For Mary Elizabeth Kane

CONTENTS

PREFACE

This book, which covers the period from Herodotus to Polybius, is introductory in nature and is aimed at A level and first-year undergraduates. It was written at the invitation of Richard Stoneman, who wanted for Greek historiography the kind of introduction W.K.C. Guthrie had provided for philosophy in his *The Greek Philosophers*, also published by Routledge. It is therefore short and without footnotes; references to the ancient sources are included within parentheses in the text. At the end are some suggestions for further reading in English.

ABBREVIATIONS

DK   H. Diels and W. Kranz (eds), (1951–1952) *Die Fragmente der Vorsokratiker* (6th edn), Berlin: Weidmann

F, FF   fragment, fragments

FGrH   F. Jacoby (ed.), (1923–1958) *Die Fragmente der griechischen Historiker*, Berlin and Leiden: E.J. Brill

T   *testimonium*

1

BEFORE HISTORY

History owed its origin chiefly to Homer, although it was one of the latest genres of literature to be created by the Greeks. Herodotus, father of history, wrote ca. 450–425 BC, considerably after the appearance of epic, lyric poetry, philosophy, tragedy and comedy, and some four hundred years, according to his own reckoning (2.53), after Homer. Why did history develop so late?

The most significant reason was that Homer's subject matter, the Trojan War and the return of Odysseus to Ithaca, was almost universally believed to concern events that really happened and persons who really existed. Homer, in short, *was* history: it did not need to be invented. What he said about events, men, the gods and most other matters was for a long time accepted as part of the traditional beliefs of the early Greeks, sometimes called the inherited conglomerate. Homer was the most important part of this inheritance, but it included Greek myths other than those he told, such as those concerning Jason, Oedipus and Minos, and poets other than Homer, such as Hesiod and the authors of the Cyclic Epics. It was only when the Greeks began to look upon their world and their cultural inheritance in a critical spirit, beginning roughly a century before Herodotus was born, that the way was open for the birth of history.

This birth, however, was difficult and long in coming because what was at issue was not the "historicity" of the broad picture in Homer— for that, as has been said, was accepted by nearly everyone—but the many improbable and miraculous elements of the *Iliad* and *Odyssey* and of other myths and sagas: the one-eyed monster Polyphemus, the battle between Achilles and the Scamander River, men who could lift ten times the weight that contemporaries could, the goddess Athena conversing with Odysseus and the like. Men began, especially under the stimulus of the early philosophers, to doubt such marvels.

1

A good many elements in Homer (and in the mythopoeic tradition generally) were thus called into question. But this was not to impugn Homer's overall version of events or to stimulate immediately the appearance of the new genre of history. Instead, the truth of Homer's accounts was salvaged by ignoring some improbabilities and glossing over others, while the chief method of dealing with the problem was rationalization. For example, King Priam of Troy would scarcely have allowed his many sons to be killed one after another over a ten-year period simply to satisfy the enjoyment of Helen by one of them, Alexander or Paris. Helen would have been handed back, and the reason she was not returned was that she was not in Troy and never had been. What is more, Homer knew this (so Herodotus 2.120). Or the reason the Greeks accompanied Agamemnon to Troy was more fear of the king's great naval power than faithfulness to their oaths to Tyndareus, Helen's father, to avenge her kidnapping (so Thucydides 1.9).

From one point of view such rationalizations may have delayed rather than accelerated the birth of history, since they were often aimed at preserving the essential integrity of Homer and the other poets. They could be (and were) applied over the entire range of the mythopoeic tradition. Only when men began to seek corroboration of the truth about men and events through the testimony of contemporaries (as well as through tangible evidence, such as monuments, documentation and the like) or through the memory of those who lived recently could a genre of writing emerge that was seen to be different from that of the early poets, standing on its own and with a character and premises special to it. Yet on this central point, which basically reduces to the difference between contemporary or near-contemporary history on the one hand and traditions about the distant past on the other, historiography throughout classical antiquity never reached a consensus. On one side were those who were content to recount the mostly rationalized legends of bygone eras, passing them off as history, and on the other those who recounted the events of the recent past chiefly on the evidence of eyewitnesses and contemporaries. There were a few who wrote vast, synoptic histories that reached from far distant days to their own age.

But it is clear that what we today consider the greatest of the ancient historians, whether of Greece or of Rome, were the writers of contemporary or near-contemporary history: Herodotus, Thucydides and Polybius in Greece; Sallust, Tacitus and Ammianus Marcellinus among the Romans (Livy, whom many would rank as a major

2

historian, is the exception). But it is instructive to note that everyone was willing to call "history" the products of both approaches: the point of dispute was over which was better or preferable. The status of far distant events, especially those enshrined in myth and legend, was therefore never really settled. If the fabulous and the improbable were removed, some believed, the residuum was deemed probable and hence historical: verisimilitude was equivalent to veracity.

It seems paradoxical to assert both that the reaction against Homer was a major stimulus to the birth of history and that the classical historians took directly from Homer their basic subject matter and the form in which they presented it. But such was the case.

First, subject matter. In the *Iliad* the dominant theme is war. The first two historians took over this topic as their own: the Persian Wars for Herodotus and the Peloponnesian War for Thucydides. Both men implicitly and sometimes explicitly compare their works with the *Iliad*. They appear to feel themselves in some measure in competition with Homer: *their* wars are more momentous, on a grander scale, or more calamitous than the Trojan conflict. To the end of antiquity historians continued to feature war prominently: for many it was a theme that dominated all else. From the *Odyssey* came a second major topic, descriptions of foreign lands and peoples: the land of the Phaeacians, Sicily of the Cyclopes, Circe's island, even the underworld. Such subject matter had its continuation in the historians: geography and landscape, flora and fauna, customs and institutions of the inhabitants. And, as in the *Odyssey*, the exotic and bizarre nature of these far-off places was particularly featured: such marvels made for entertaining reading, while the strangeness of remote lands gave the Greeks a sense of their own identity and special place in the world. Herodotus, Theopompus, historians of Alexander the Great and Polybius devoted sizable portions of their works to such descriptions. Even Thucydides, despite his intense and restricted focus, includes, for example, a section on the cities and peoples of Sicily (6.2–5).

Second, the form in which history was cast. Homer's epics are essentially a narrative of events: accounts of what people did and what people said, often richly detailed and highly circumstantial. Speeches are a major element, usually presented in direct discourse and some-times cast as sustained dialogue. The aim was to recreate before the reader's (or listener's) eyes a sense of vivid immediacy, a feeling of "you-are-there." This technique was taken over by Herodotus and his successors; to the end of antiquity it remained the hallmark of historical writing. A modern reader, not expecting to find such writing in a history, may be startled in the first pages of Herodotus, for example, to find himself in the boudoir of a Lydian queen, peeking out from behind a door as she removes her clothing piece by piece in preparation for bed. Awaiting her in the bed is the king, and peering from behind the door is the captain of his bodyguard. The captain, we learn, is there under pain of death should he refuse to look upon the queen naked. And it is the king who has put him up to it! This sort of thing seems somehow "unhistorical" to the modern reader, but in antiquity it was the very stuff of history.

It is also important to realize what classical historiography essentially was not: not an account of abiding conditions and institutions, whether military, religious or political; not an analysis of social classes, economic factors or cultural achievements. Such topics did appear in histories, to be sure, but in the form of prefaces and digressions, often brief. The overall framework was a narrative of events, without which these other subjects, which most people today consider central to historical writing, could find no place. When an author wished to write an extended account of topics like the constitutions of states or military tactics he sometimes composed a separate monograph rather than making it a subordinate part of a larger history. A few historians, notably Theopompus and Polybius, did include sizable digressions in their histories, but both they and their readers were well aware of the intrusive and separable nature of what plainly were lengthy departures from the main business of history.

History was therefore a literary enterprise above all, the imaginative creation of its author. It was to be written in the language of its creator: quotation of documents and direct transcriptions had little place. Only rarely would a historian admit into his text the verbatim language of others. Moreover, just as Trojans, Polyphemus and other non-Greeks all speak beautiful (and metrical) Greek in Homer, so Persians, Lydians and other non-Greeks uniformly talk in the distinctive Ionic dialect of Herodotus. No one for a moment thought that such direct speech was what was actually said. The same principle holds for descriptions like that of the queen disrobing: the half-open door, the chair on which she placed her garments, the captain peering from behind the door and so forth. Clearly the scene is an imaginative recreation.

Why did the Greeks conceive of history in this way? Homer's influence is an important reason, as has been said. But there is perhaps a more significant one which, though obvious, needs to be stressed: in antiquity there was virtually no way that words or actions could be exactly reproduced after the fact, even immediately after the fact. We in our world are so used to having available to us on-the-spot reports, verbatim transcriptions, photographs, tape and video recordings, and to having libraries and other repositories where such information may be consulted, that we sometimes fall into the trap of supposing that the ancients had the option of whether to base their writings on primary documents and that they rejected it for literary or other "anti-historical" reasons—or even out of ignorance as to the real worth of such resources. This, of course, was not the case. They did not think in such terms: the precise details and exact words they recorded did not represent what was literally done or said because they could not.

Nor, I think, would they have desired the option, even had it been available. History was the creation of the historian, not a mirror he held up to a subject that had an objective and independent existence apart from himself and which he might transfer faithfully to the page. There is, in fact, no real word in Greek for history in the sense of "the past" or "the subject matter of written accounts." A word like *historía*, for example, meant either the written accounts themselves, or the process of inquiry that led to the creation of such accounts. In sum, history existed in men's minds and on the written page: it was a mental construct that the historian put in permanent literary form.

The ancient historians seem to have been quite content with their inheritance from Homer. After the first historians had adopted the essential form which his epic poems took—a narrative of events, together with direct speeches—the proper mold for the genre of history was forever set. No one thereafter, at least no serious or substantial historian, deviated greatly from the format. Variations and elaborations on it were essayed, but the basic form abided. Thucydides, for example, the "severest" and seemingly most modern of the ancient historians, relied so completely on the narrative-speech format and admitted so few digressions that one critic in later antiquity complained of the lack of variety and pleasurable diversion in his work.

From what has been said it should be clear that the classical historians had a different conception of historical truth than we do today. Because every account of an event or speech was necessarily an imaginative reconstruction, there was from our modern viewpoint a great deal of "untruth" in ancient historiography. Moreover, as one moved backward in time from contemporary and near-contemporary history, the more one had to rely on the accounts of others and,

5

correspondingly, the less opportunity the historian had to verify reports by seeking out eyewitnesses, participants and those who had access to them. Polybius, for example (4.2), declared that his history would be largely restricted to the lifetimes of himself and his father: to go further back would be to write a report based on the hearsay of others.

The history of times long past was particularly problematic: myths and legends frequently had variant versions and tended to attract bizarre and miraculous elements. When confronted with material of this sort, historians had a range of options. Some simply refused to deal with them, or dealt with them in a very limited way (Thucydides is an example, although he believed that a character like Minos was a real person who played a significant role in history: 1.8). Others, aware of the uncertainty of the subject matter, included such material, but with disclaimers: they were bound to report what people said, but not to believe it. Still others resorted to extensive rationalization: by eliminating the miraculous and improbable, they believed that they had come close to the truth. For example, Dionysius of Halicarnassus, a Greek historian of the Roman period, presents two versions of the tenth labor of Hercules (1.39–42). The first he labels the mythical one: namely, that the hero (soon to become a god) slew with his club the triple-headed monster Geryon in far-off Spain and stole his cattle. The second is "the truer version," Dionysius tells us, one "which those adopt who have written up his deeds in historical form:" Heracles was really a highly successful general at the head of an army that roamed over the Mediterranean world deposing tyrants and doing other good deeds. He was in Spain to conquer it, not to steal cattle.

There was, then, no hard and fast line between truth and untruth, between what was reliable and what was not. Rather, a "sliding scale" obtained between the extremes. Some have declared that ancient historiography was more like a historical novel than a modern history. There is some truth to this. But at bottom there is a fundamental difference: the novelist freely creates characters and episodes as his story requires; the historian cannot be anywhere near so free—or at least he should not. He is bound to follow what his sources, both oral and written report: his "imaginative reconstruction" must be based on them and them alone. Yet, as has been said, the further back he goes in time, the less detailed, more conflicting and sometimes more improbable the information in these sources tends to become—and, correspondingly, the more his accounts resemble the historical novel, or sometimes a miraculous adventure tale.

In a famous passage in the *Poetics* (9) Aristotle discusses the difference between history and poetry (he is thinking chiefly of tragedy and epic). The distinction is not between prose and verse, he argues: if Herodotus' work were in meter, it would still be a kind of history. The chief difference is that poetry concerns what a certain type of person would do in accordance with probability or necessity. Poetry expresses the universal: what may happen. History, on the other hand, concerns the particular—what Alcibiades did or suffered. Poetry is more philosophical and more valuable than history in Aristotle's eyes because of this universalizing quality. Aristotle seems to be implying that in real life improbable, fortuitous and irrational things are apt to happen: the historian has no choice but to record them, whereas the poet is both selective and inventive in what he writes, doing so in accordance with what a particular type of person is likely to do, or must do.

Few have been satisfied with Aristotle's definition of history here, chiefly because of what he fails to say. The greatest of the Greek historians, as will appear in what follows, were much concerned with "universals." They looked not so much to individuals, however, as to groups: from the mass of particulars that constitute their subject they derived certain principles of cause and reaction which, they believed, possessed general and universal application. In this same chapter Aristotle says that since most characters in tragedy were real people, the audience will believe in them because "what has happened is clearly possible, for it would not have happened were it impossible." And he adds: "If he chooses as his subject events that have happened, he is none the less a poet. For nothing prevents some things that have happened from being the sort of events that are likely and possible, and in this respect he is their poet" (*poiêtês* in Greek means both "poet" and "maker/creator").

Another important influence on the birth of history, in addition to Homer, was philosophy. The first philosophers, known as the Pre-Socratics (Socrates died in 399 BC), most of whom are preserved in fragments quoted in later writers, began to look at the world in a new spirit, rejecting simple acceptance of traditional beliefs (the "inherited conglomerate") in favor of critical inquiry and creative explanations. Most of these early philosophers came from Ionia: that is, the Greek cities situated on the littoral of the Aegean Sea in Asia Minor (modern Turkey), the same area from which Herodotus came. Some of them rejected or modified the typical Greek view of the gods as directly influencing the workings of nature and the activities of man: for example, that the rainbow was the path by which the goddess Iris descended to earth, or that Poseidon caused earthquakes by striking the land with his trident or that a giant lay imprisoned beneath Mt Etna in Sicily, causing tremors and eruptions as he struggled to be free.

Instead, many of these early thinkers began to seek natural explanations by inquiring into the working of the phenomenal world and by formulating theories to explain what they saw. Some of their observations and deductions are quite startling. For example, Anaximander of Miletus in the sixth century noticed certain mammalian characteristics of a species of shark; from this and other observations he postulated that terrestial life originated in mud as seawater evaporated in the sun (*DK* 12A11, 30). Or Xenophanes of Colophon, who lived in the late sixth and early fifth centuries, observed the fossils of sea creatures and land plants embedded in rocks, from which he deduced that at one time these living things had been caught in sea mud, which then dried and became rock (*DK* 21A33). He also maintained that the rainbow was not the goddess Iris, but simply a colored cloud (*DK* 12F32).

Yet these men were not scientists. Their inquiries were sporadic and random, nor were they concerned to explain the particulars of nature in any systematic way. Rather, their aim was to discover the general principles that underlay the particulars of the phenomenal world. From relatively few observations they intuited these principles by an imaginative leap: what was important was the theory, not the individual observations or deductions.

Change was the phenomenon that most fascinated them. On the one hand, all things were in a state of flux: no stone was so hard that it did not eventually wear away; stars, sun and moon were ever on the move in the heavens above. On the other hand, the changes that regulated the larger workings of nature followed fixed and predictable patterns: the passing of the seasons, the phases of the moon, the growth and decay of plant and animal life. Hence a great paradox: in one sense all things change, and in another they stay the same. Change is unchanging. And it is predictable: for example, Thales of Miletus, reckoned the father of philosophy, predicted the eclipse of the sun that occurred on 28 May 585 BC during a battle between the Lydians and the Medes (Herodotus 1.74).

There must be, these early thinkers felt, certain principles that underlie our phenomenal world. Moreover, when we look at the vast complexity of all the particulars around us, we see that each class of thing has its own nature—characteristics that make it what it is and not something else. This special nature the Greeks called its *physis*. Each thing, moreover has its particular place in the world; to it belongs a set portion or lot (*moira*), within which it operates and beyond which it must not or cannot go. This is one's lot or destiny, presided over by the goddess or goddesses of fate (Moira, Moirai). Moreover, all things are connected to and interact with one another in fixed and predictable ways. In short, the world exhibits above all stability and order, the Greek word for which was *kosmos*. Rather quickly *kosmos* became applied to the universe itself, since in their eyes it was the embodiment of order.

The theories proposed by these early philosophers were as various as were their personalities. No one of them appears to have agreed with another, and in no way did they form a school of thought. Some fixed on substances as the underlying "first principle," such as water or air (Thales, Anaximenes); others on a combination of them, such as fire, air, water and earth (Empedocles); still others on abstract forces such as the Infinite or numbers (Anaximander, Pythagoras). One of the most interesting was Heraclitus of Ephesus, who flourished around 500 BC. The universe is in perpetual flux, he maintained. His most famous dictum was, "It is not possible to step into the same river twice, for different waters ever flow upon you" (*DK* 22B12, 91). Change is a constant shifting between extremes, like the pendulum of a clock. The world therefore is a battleground between opposing forces: "One should know that everything comes about by conflict and necessity," he said (*DK* 22B80). But this conflict is what keeps the world in balance and ensures *kosmos*: "Men do not understand that what is at variance with itself is in agreement. It is a harmony of opposite tensions, like that of the bow and the lyre" (*DK* 22B51). Or again, "That which is in opposition fits together; from differing elements comes the most beautiful harmony" (*DK* 22B8). Heraclitus earned himself the sobriquet "The Obscure" in antiquity for these and other sayings, such as "In changing it is at rest" (*DK* 22B84a) and "The way up and the way down is one and the same" (*DK* 22B60). He meant, of course, that for every action there is a reaction, and that together they constitute a unitary process.

These early philosophers do not seem to have influenced significantly the first historians, Herodotus and Thucydides, in an immediate or direct way. Yet without them, it is doubtful that history could have come into being, for to them are owed the following: first, critical and analytical thinking; second, observation and inquiry into the world about them; third, a comprehensive view of the universe, which they looked upon not piecemeal but as an integrated whole in which certain abiding principles operated; fourth, an interest in the phenomenon of change, for just as nature is subject to change, so are humankind and human activities—which is what history is all about.

A third impetus to the birth of history, in addition to Homer and the Pre-Socratic philosophers, were the so-called logographers or *logopoioi* (sing. *logopoios*), of whom Hecataeus of Miletus was the most important. *Logopoios* differentiated the writer from an *epopoios*: a "prose-maker" versus an "epic-maker" (cf. Herodotus 2.143, 120). *Logographos*, virtually a synonym of *logopoios*, was a writer of *logoi* (sing. *logos*). *Logos* in Greek has a wide range of meanings, including story, account, description, explanation, argument and reasoning. It is an extremely elastic term, therefore. A *logographos* could write on almost any subject, whether fact or fiction, but did so in prose. Toward the end of the fifth century BC it began to take on negative connotations on occasion: a teller of tall tales.

The creation of prose literature is a poorly understood subject in Greek literary history, chiefly because prose works before Herodotus survive only in fragmentary quotations in later writers. It is difficult to judge fully what the causes were for the growing popularity of prose in the course of the sixth and fifth centuries BC and why some genres, especially philosophy, made the shift from poetry to prose (Anaximander, mentioned above, wrote the first prose tract ca. 546 BC). Part of the reason seems to be that prose was increasingly viewed as the proper vehicle to expound specialized subjects relating to the contemporary world, such as travel, medicine, physical science, speech writing and the like.

Yet behind Hecataeus and the other logographers lay a long process within the mythopoeic tradition itself that prepared the way for them. The process was fueled by historical impulses—or so they seem to us: namely, a desire to put myths and legends into a temporal sequence, to synchronize them and then to construct genealogies that would connect the persons of mythology to men of contemporary Greece.

First, there was a desire for continuity: what preceded and followed the great epics of Homer? Hence the Cyclic Epics arose, composed by a variety of poets between Homer (ca. 800 BC) and the middle of the sixth century BC. The cycle begins with the marriage of Heaven and Earth in primeval bliss and carries through to the final settlement of Odysseus' family after his death.

Next came the desire for synchronization: when, for example, did the many legends concerning the Greek city of Thebes (the story of Oedipus is one) occur in relation to the events recounted in the *Iliad* and *Odyssey*? A Theban cycle was thus created and fixed in time before the Trojan conflict. In this process problems and impossibilities were discovered, and steps taken to correct them. For example, by tradition the poet Orpheus was a member of Jason's crew of the *Argo* that sailed in search of the Golden Fleece. But when synchronization showed that Orpheus must have lived much earlier than Jason, he was struck from the ship's roster and another recruited in his place.

The final step in "historicizing" myths was the creation of genealogies (which naturally helped in putting the separate myths in sequence and in synchronizing them). For example, Homer appropriately was shown to have descended from Orpheus, the first poet. More important, these mythic genealogies, which began with gods, demigods and heroes, were brought down and connected to aristocratic families of present-day Greece, most of whom apparently could boast such illustrious descent. Hecataeus, for instance, traced his ancestry to a god in the sixteenth generation, and it appears that Herodotus too may have had a similar genealogy to tell, had he cared to (2.143). The importance of such genealogies for reconstructing the history of Greece in the seventh and sixth centuries BC was great. Each city state had its own system of dating: e.g. annual archons in Athens, ephors in Sparta (both being titles of magistrates), priestesses of Hera in Argos (see Thucydides 2.2). With no widely known or accepted system of dating in existence, the establishing of a particular date that would be recognized by most or all Greeks was wellnigh impossible. Genealogies at least helped to sort out persons and events in particular families and in the cities from which they came; synchronizing genealogical charts helped the process somewhat further.

Thus the mythopoeic tradition after a time became codified, so to speak, and presented the appearance of a historical past. The best known example is the *Theogony* of Hesiod, who either was a contemporary of Homer or lived slightly later. Hesiod begins his poem by recounting the most primeval myths: the union of Earth and Chaos under the influence of Love (Eros), which produced Uranus, who in turn begot Kronos. Kronos then begot Zeus, who together with his siblings begot still more gods and goddesses, who in turn descended to earth and sired children by mortal partners. The last two lines of the *Theogony* allude to a lost work, the "Catalogue of [Mortal] Women," which may have originally been appended to the *Theogony*. From these

11

unions the great families of Greece traced their descent: the primal past was thus linked to the present in an unbroken line.

In his other surviving poem, *Works and Days*, Hesiod enunciates the first ancient view of history as a whole, the Five Ages of the World: Gold, Silver, Bronze, the Age of Heroes and finally Iron. As the metals indicate, humankind's history is represented as one of progressive deterioration and decline, coming down to the present Age of Iron. The Age of Heroes is clearly an intrusion into an older sequence based on metals. No doubt the intrusion was at least partly the result of chronological schemes and synchronization: when it was realized that the heroes of Homer, such as Achilles, Agamemnon and Odysseus, would have to be placed in a mere Age of Bronze, a special slot for them was inserted that interrupted the decline.

But the mythopoeic tradition and the new mythography based on it did not escape criticism from skeptics, especially some of the philosophers. Xenophanes, for example, rejected the view of the gods as having human shape or behaving dishonorably: "Homer and Hesiod have attributed to the gods all things that are disgraceful and blameworthy among mankind: theft, adultery and deceiving one another" (*DK* 21B11–12). Heraclitus in fact asserted that Homer deserved a stout thrashing (*DK* 22B42). Xenophanes went on to brand Greek myths in general as "ancient fictions," mentioning as examples the battles of the Titans and those among the Giants (*DK* 21B1). New standards of criticism arose, that have been summed up in this way: "What was possible once is possible still, and what is incredible now is incredible always" (Bury 1909: 11). One result of this credo was to replace literal epiphanies of gods upon earth with indirect communication: oracles, dreams and prophecies.

The way was thus prepared for the advent of the logographers. Unfortunately, with the exception of Hecataeus, next to nothing is known of any of them: some names and titles survive, plus a few fragments. One or two are suspected of not having existed at all (e.g. Dionysius of Miletus), while others may have written somewhat later than Herodotus (e.g. Xanthus the Lydian). The subjects on which they wrote included genealogies (Acusilaus of Argos), mythography (Pherecydes of Syros) and geography (Scylax of Caryanda). Charon of Lampsacus wrote *Persica* and *Hellenica*, which, like his other works, were probably descriptions of the peoples and places of Persia and Greece, respectively, rather than histories proper.

Herodotus cites none of these writers, and there is no evidence that he used any of them, cited or not. He names a single prose writer among his sources, Hecataeus of Miletus. Hecataeus, a contemporary of Xenophanes, lived in the later sixth and early fifth centuries BC. At the beginning of the Ionian Revolt that began the Persian Wars (499 BC), when Miletus was debating whether to revolt from Persian domination, Herodotus says Hecataeus alone advised against it because of Persia's great power (5.36), but when no one agreed, he urged that the city aim to control the sea through monies realized from nearby temple treasures. Herodotus also records another piece of neglected advice that Hecataeus gave near the end of the revolt, when it was in collapse (5.125). The source of this information is probably Hecataeus himself, since disregarded advice is likely to come from the person who gave it.

Hecataeus began one of his works, *Genealogies*, with these words (*FGrH* 1F1): "Hecataeus of Miletus says this: I write what seems to me to be true, for the stories (*logoi*) of the Greeks appear to me to be many and laughable." A combative and critical spirit is evidenced at once, rather in the spirit of Xenophanes; it was possibly in this work that Hecataeus claimed to trace his ancestry back to a god in the sixteenth generation. In another work, *Periêgêsis* or "Journey Around the World," he described the peoples and cities of the Mediterranean and Black Sea littoral, although there are fragments that refer to such far-off places as India. It contained a mix of critical reportage, rationalization, aetiology and outright gullibility. An example of rationalization is the shifting of the lair of the monster Geryon from an island in the Ocean off the coast of Spain to the district of Epirus in northwestern Greece, thus sparing Heracles and the stolen cattle an arduous trek that would entail crossing numerous water obstacles, to say nothing of the Pyrenees, Alps and Balkans. Geryon, moreover, is not a triple-headed monster in this version, but the local king; even so, Heracles' driving the cattle from Epirus to southern Greece was, Hecataeus assures us, no slight achievement (*FGrH* 1F26). As for gullibility, Hecataeus reported that in Egypt there was an island that "floats, sails about and moves" (*FGrH* 1F305). Herodotus, without naming Hecataeus, slyly says of the same locale (2.156): "The island is said by the Egyptians to float. Now I myself did not see it sailing about or being moved, and I was surprised to hear that an island actually floats." Save for an account of his role in the Ionian Revolt, there is little evidence that Hecataeus said much, if anything, about the histories of the places he described in his *Periêgêsis*. Peoples, places, customs and the like were the focus of his attention. Damastes of Sigeum, however, a logographer contemporary with Herodotus, does seem to have written on historical matters in a work entitled *Events in Greece*.

The way thus lay open for the invention of history by Herodotus. It was long .in coming, as has been argued, because Homer and the mythopoeic tradition both inspired and deterred history's birth, inspiring it through the themes of war and travel and through a narrative of vivid description and direct speech, deterring it because most people believed that what Homer wrote was history, in the sense that his subject matter concerned real events and real people. Only when the early philosophers and the logographers ventured to look at the mythopoeic tradition in a critical spirit was the avenue open for critical history of the sort Herodotus wrote. Indeed, criticism of one's predecessors was to prove a hallmark of ancient Greek historiography throughout its existence. The acrid smoke of rivalry, rejection and rebuke filled a battlefield of conflicting credos, bruised feelings and swollen egos. Xenophanes had mocked the myths as "ancient fictions." Hecataeus decried the "many and laughable stories of the Greeks." Heraclitus said in turn (*DK* 22B40): "Knowing a lot does not teach a man to have sense. It certainly did not teach Hesiod and Pythagoras, or, for that matter, Xenophanes and Hecataeus."

2

HERODOTUS AND *HISTORÍA*

It was said before that Herodotus' subject is the Persian Wars (499–479 BC), but this is not completely accurate. Here is his proem:

> Herodotus of Halicarnassus herein puts on display the result of his inquiries so that man's past may not fade into oblivion over time nor the great and amazing deeds displayed by both Greeks and barbarians be without renown, with particular attention to the reason they went to war with one another.

There is no specific mention here of Persians or the wars with Persia; the clash, rather, is on a grander scale: between barbarians and Greeks, between East and West. Yet the wars with Persia take up roughly the last half of the work and are recounted in much more detail than is any other sequence of events. They clearly are the focus and the climax of the *Histories* as a whole, but they do not constitute the whole.

The division of the work into nine books was not Herodotus' doing, but probably that of the scholars of the great library at Alexandria in the third century BC (at some point in antiquity they were named for the nine Muses; the chapter divisions were made in the Renaissance). The overall plan is relatively simple: the work follows the Persian Empire monarch by monarch from its inception to the extraordinary defeat inflicted upon it by the Greeks. Book 1 concerns the founder of Persian power, Cyrus (ca. 559–529 BC), with particular emphasis on Cyrus' defeat of King Croesus of Lydia and how the Greek cities of Ionia that Croesus had conquered passed into Persian control. Cyrus' conquest of Babylon and his death fighting the backward Massagetae are also prominently featured. Book 2 and the first third of 3 concern Egypt, culminating in the subjugation of that country by Cyrus' successor, Cambyses (529–521 BC). The brief occupation of the throne by the "false Smerdis," a member of the priestly cast of the Magi, is

15

quickly followed by the reign of Darius (521–486 BC), covering the rest of Book 3 through Book 6. Book 4 features Darius' expedition against the Scythians in south Russia, the first part of Book 5 describes Persia's conquest of the north Aegean area, the rest of 5 and all of 6 describe the outbreak of the Ionian Revolt in 499 BC and its consequences over the next nine years. The revolt failed, but Darius was incensed that two cities in the Greek homeland had dared to help the cause of the Ionians, Athens and nearby Eretria on the island of Euboea. Darius determined to punish them, but his first expedition suffered disaster in a storm at sea off Mt Athos in the north Aegean (Book 6). The second, avoiding Athos altogether, moved across the central Aegean, but met a stunning defeat at Marathon at the hands of the Athenians (490 BC, Book 6). Darius soon died, and his successor Xerxes (485–465 BC) determined to avenge Marathon. He mounted a mighty expedition to Greece (consisting of some five and a half million men, claims Herodotus), winning a victory at the Battle of Thermopylae (480 BC, Book 7), but suffering a humiliating defeat by sea at the Battle of Salamis (480 BC, Book 8) and again on land in the Battles of Plataea and Mycale (479, Book 9). The *Histories* end with the triumphant liberation of Ionian cities from Persian control.

The overall plan, then, is straightforward and easy to follow, though obviously it is done on a grand scale both in time and space. Herodotus' method of narration, however, much of it borrowed from Homer, is to digress frequently, sometimes at great length, but to bring the story back to the point of departure before continuing with the main narrative ("ring composition"). The past histories of many Greek city states are narrated in this way: for example, two paired segments on Athens and Sparta are given in Books 1 and 5 (yet there are also many other flashbacks on Athenian and Spartan matters elsewhere in the *Histories*). As Persia conquers or comes into contact with different lands and peoples in the course of acquiring her empire, Herodotus often stops to give an account of these places: topography, climate, flora, fauna, natural resources, customs, past history and the like. Some of the major areas are Lydia, Babylon and the Massagetae in Book 1; Egypt in Book 2 and the first part of 3—a huge digression taking up about a ninth of the work; the Greek island of Samos in Book 3; Scythia and the city state of Cyrene in North Africa in Book 4; and Thrace in the first part of Book 5. Once the account of the Ionian Revolt begins at 5.28 excursuses on peoples other than Greeks and Persians become much reduced. Yet Herodotus' curiosity is piqued by so many subjects that it seems almost anything can qualify for inclusion. For example, in describing how horses and mules react to the cold climate of Scythia in south Russia, he is reminded of the fact that mules for some unknown reason cannot be bred in the Greek city-state of Elis. As he begins his brief review of this surprising fact he remarks disarmingly, "From the start my narrative (*logos*) has quite naturally led to digressions" (4.30).

One of the most discussed questions among students of Herodotus concerns how we may suppose he came to invent history. Did he, for example, begin his inquiries in the manner of Hecataeus in his *Periêgêsis*, writing up the results of travels to places such as Lydia, Babylon, Egypt, Scythia, Cyrene and Thrace, but realizing at some point along the way how all of the material could be integrated into a single account, with the rise of Persia's empire and its defeat at the hands of the Greeks as the unifying theme? Some have not unreasonably supposed that this was the road that led to him history. Others reverse the process: Herodotus first wrote up an account of Xerxes' invasion of Greece (Books 7–9: 480–479 BC) but then decided in a huge preamble to describe the origin and growth of Persian power in the eighty years from ca. 560 BC to the start of the invasion. Still others believe Herodotus had the grand scheme in his head from the beginning, writing the *Histories* from start to finish substantially as we now see it.

Certainly sections of the *Histories* seem to have enjoyed an existence rather independent of the rest, if only because the work must have become known in part through recitations, which could have embraced only comparatively small pieces of the whole on each occasion. Herodotus refers to sections of his history as *logoi*, or accounts. One would imagine in any event that such a lengthy work must have been composed in sections and perhaps over many years. Certainly 3.80–82 was written before 6.43, for Herodotus assures us in the latter passage that, despite the doubts of some Greeks, three prominent Persians at the death of the false Smerdis, as he had described earlier, really did debate among themselves the merits of monarchy, oligarchy and democracy, and that one of them championed the virtues of democracy. There is a similar back reference from 7.93 to 1.173. Moreover, certain sections of the *Histories* have seemed to some scholars to be rather poorly fitted into their present places. The section on Egypt, for example, seems overlong in comparison to the rest of the work and to have certain other characteristics that mark it off, such as greater contentiousness against those with whom Herodotus disagrees and the absence of speeches of any length. And there are numerous smaller sections that some have felt to be awkwardly fitted into their contexts.

Although one would like to know how Herodotus conceived of the idea of history, the text as we have it is susceptible of many explanations of how it came to take its present form; in fact, the advocates of quite different theories sometimes use the same passages to support their conflicting views. Some have wondered whether the work was completely finished, for although Herodotus promises to give us an Assyrian *logos* it does not survive (1.106, 184). Did he fail to write it up, or has it dropped from our text as if it had been part of a series of rather detachable *logoi*? He also promises to tell us of the fate of the traitor Ephialtes, but never does (7.213). Despite these unfulfilled promises, most readers consider the *Histories* substantially if not fully finished. Certainly the concluding anecdote has all the marks of finality and closure (9.122).

Something should also be said of Herodotus' language and style. He writes in the Ionic dialect, but with the admixture of other forms and of poeticisms. His style, on the level of sentence structure, frequently employs simple connectives and straightforward linearity: parataxis, as opposed to the periodic sentence that relies on subordination to give it a rounded, architectural effect. Aristotle called it the "strung-along" style (*Rhetoric* 3.9.1–2=1409a). It is a mirror of Herodotus' method of narration as well: one story leads to another in a seemingly artless, "tacked-on" manner. Much of Herodotus' considerable charm comes from just these devices, both in language and in narration. Yet it is deceptive: beneath the surface of apparent naivety, unexpected depths lurk—depths of wit, irony, pathos and acuity. Moreover, Herodotus is capable of writing quite elaborate periods when he wishes, and the meaning of many seemingly simple sentences turns out to be allusive and even elusive on close inspection. Edward Gibbon once said that Herodotus sometimes writes for children and sometimes for philosophers. He might have added that on occasion he writes for both at the same time.

Little is known about the life of Herodotus, and much of that little can be found or deduced from the *Histories* themselves. Still, it is clear that Herodotus came from the city of Halicarnassus in Asia Minor (modern Bodrum in Turkey), which in his earliest years was part of the Persian Empire. The names of his father (Lyxes) and of a cousin or uncle (Panyassis) are not Greek but Carian, the Carians being the native people in the hinterland of Halicarnassus. Herodotus was of mixed blood, it would appear, as were, inscriptions show, many of his fellow townsmen. Halicarnassus, in fact, was a city on many margins: of the Persian Empire, of Ionia (to the south the Dorian dialect was spoken, and Dorians were said originally to have founded the city) and of the non-Greek hinterland. Herodotus' cosmopolitanism and his openness to foreign cultures may owe much to the situation of his native city. Panyassis, sometimes called the last of the epic poets, wrote a long poem on the deeds of Heracles and another (not in epic meter) on Ionia. Early in his life Herodotus appears to have been driven into exile by a political upheaval at Halicarnassus in which Panyassis lost his life. We hear that he spent some years both on the nearby island of Samos and at Athens, and his detailed knowledge of these places in the *Histories* confirms this. We hear also that he joined the panhellenic foundation of the colony of Thurii in south Italy, which was settled in 444/443 BC under the sponsorship of Athens.

Such meager facts did not satisfy men later in antiquity: invention and embroidery filled the void of ignorance. Herodotus was said to have recited a part of the *Histories* at Athens and to have received a reward for it (which is likely enough). To add greater precision, the absurdly high sum of ten talents was later fixed on the the amount of the reward, the consequence of Athenian delight at being favorably depicted in the *Histories*. The theme was then given a further twist: Herodotus went to Corinth and when he demanded money for presenting that city in a positive light the Corinthians refused, whereupon the historian retaliated by including a number of anti-Corinthian stories in his work. Thebes was added to the list of those Herodotus unfairly traduced, the cause being in this case the refusal of the Thebans to allow him to open a school there. Now that Herodotus was reciting his work in Athens, his tour was extended to include the Olympic games, where all of Greece could hear him. Then came the final touch: the young Thucydides was also at Olympia; he sat at the master's feet and burst into tears on hearing Herodotus' words, whereupon the grand old man complimented the youth "because his spirit was roused by learning."

Such fictions fleshed out the few secure facts of Herodotus' life. Since the year of birth of most fifth-century writers was unknown, a common method of supplying one was to select an event dated to what was thought to be the prime of the writer's life and to count back forty years. In Herodotus' case, the founding of Thurii in 444/443 supplied the fixed date; hence the year of birth was assigned to 484. From everything we can tell, this seems a good guess (but not so for

Thucydides: the outbreak of the Peloponnesian War in 431 gave a birthdate for him of 471, which is too early). The last securely datable events to which Herodotus refers in the *Histories* occurred in the first years of the Peloponnesian War. His death, therefore, may have come in the mid- or late 420s BC. By 425 the preface to his history (1.1–5) was well enough known for the comic poet Aristophanes to parody it in his play *The Acharnians* (Sophocles also seems to have borrowed from Herodotus 3.119 in writing *Antigone* 904–920, produced in 441). Where he died is a question: perhaps at Thurii, although some are inclined to think he returned to Athens before the outbreak of the Peloponnesian War and that he died there.

Most significant for Herodotus' life were his travels. It is clear that he knew firsthand much of the eastern Mediterranean and the Black Sea. Some of the places he visited were Sardis, the capital of Lydia in Asia Minor; the Phoenician city of Tyre (2.49); Egypt as far as the first cataract on the Nile at Elephantine (modern Aswan); the Black Sea, calculating its length and breadth (4.86) and penetrating to a site four days journey up the Hypanis (Bug) River in south Russia (4.52); and, naturally, many places in Greece, including the oracular shrine of Apollo at Delphi. Overland travel was difficult for most people in antiquity, and this seems generally true for Herodotus; yet he appears to have reached the Euphrates River, where he describes collapsible boats that were floated with their cargos downstream to Babylon, then folded up and taken back to be reused for another journey (1.194). He mentions the western Mediterranean infrequently, which is natural, given his focus on Persia and the East in general. Yet he makes some elementary errors of western geography (see below), which suggests that he did not know it well.

So extensive were these travels and so keen was Herodotus' interest in navigation, types of boats and articles of commerce that some have supposed, not unreasonably, that he made his living as a trader after being driven from Halicarnassus. However that may be, the information he gathered on these travels supplied the great bulk of the material for the *Histories*. Of written sources, Hecataeus, as has been said, was the only prose writer that he names or seems to have used; of the some twenty references to individual poets or poets in general, only a very few could have supplied him with extensive information (the *Arimaspea* of Aristeas was one of them: 4.13–16). He almost certainly had a number of Persian informants who supplied him with material; some of it is quite full and detailed, and seems to have derived from "official" sources, such as the tribute list under Darius (3.89–96), the course of the Royal Road from Sardis to the Persian capital at Susa (5.52–54) and the roster of troops and ships that Xerxes brought from Asia to Europe (7.59–99).

There is no evidence, however, that he knew any language other than Greek (for example, despite his Persian friends, some of what he was told or inferred about their language looks to be in error: 1.139). He was thus at the mercy of foreign informants who communicated directly with him in Greek or through interpreters. Sometimes he was misled or jumped to a wrong conclusion. For example, an interpreter told him that an inscription cut into the facing of the pyramid of Cheops mentioned radishes, onions and garlic. This Herodotus took to be what was needed to feed the laborers: "I remember quite distinctly that the interpreter who read me the inscription said the 1,600 talents of silver was the amount expended" (2.125). Whatever the nature of the inscription, Egyptologists are sure of one thing: the interpreter led Herodotus up the garden path.

The vast bulk of the information, therefore, had to be gathered through firsthand inquiry: by autopsy and by listening to what people had to say about themselves, their culture and their history. This achievement was by itself astounding, covering as it did a span of time beginning some hundred years before and ending when Herodotus was a young child, and encompassing a huge area that dozens of modern countries now occupy. That Herodotus was able to gather most of his information by personal inquiry and to see how it fitted together in one grand historical scheme is one of the great achievements of his or any other age. His invention of history was not some tentative and blinkered affair, therefore, but one of astonishing scope and complexity.

The word for "inquiry" that Herodotus uses is *historía* (Ionic dialect *historíē*). The noun and its verb (*historeô*) denote on-the-spot inquiry of what one sees and hears. In Herodotus it is the process or method of investigation rather than the result. Only in the fourth century and later did the word take on the specific meaning of "a written account of man's past activities." In the fifth century *historía* denoted intellectual inquiry of all sorts, although then and later it became especially associated with the systematic inquiry into the phenomenal world, particularly scientific subjects (compare Aristotle's "History of Animals" or a modern Museum of Natural History). In Homer the related noun *istôr* means one who judges the facts in a dispute or an umpire present to witness a contest and determine the winner.

Because he had to gather most of his information by personal inquiry during his travels, Herodotus was acutely conscious that the reliability of his sources and of the information they supplied was quite variable. He often specifies his informants (e.g. the priests at the temple of Apollo at Delphi or at particular temples in Egypt) and occasionally identifies individuals by name. He frequently lets us know of conflicting versions and interpretations he was given: we can thus glimpse something of the process that led to the finished composition. Often he was not satisfied simply to record what a particular source said; he liked to check its accuracy by consulting other people on the same subject. A remarkable instance concerns the cult of Heracles, a figure in whom he shows much interest (2.43–44: cf. the epic poem on Heracles by his relative Panyassis). At Memphis in Egypt he learned that Heracles had been worshipped there for 1,700 years (and was not, therefore, as the Greeks thought, a mortal who lived in relatively recent times and became a god). He then travelled to Tyre in Phoenicia "wanting to get as reliable information as I could;" there the temple of Heracles was claimed to be 2,300 years old. At Tyre he also saw a temple dedicated to the Thasian Heracles; so Herodotus travelled to the Greek island of Thasos in the north Aegean, where he saw a temple that was said to have been founded by the Phoenicians during their search for the kidnapped Europa. Even this temple, Herodotus was told, was founded five generations before the Greeks say Heracles appeared on earth. "These results of my inquiries (*historeô*) show clearly that Heracles is a very ancient god," he concludes. He had travelled the breadth of the Mediterranean in his attempt to verify what he had been told in Memphis.

Herodotus' concern to identify the type and quality of his sources is strikingly shown in his long account of Egypt (2.1–3.38). He explicitly divides it into three parts. To us moderns it is natural to see these divisions as based on subject matter: the land and people of Egypt (2.1–98), early history of the pharaohs (2.99–146) and recent history (2.147–3.38). But this is not how Herodotus formulates the question. At the first break he says (2.99): "Up to this point my account has been based on observation, inference and inquiry (*historíê*), but from now on I will report what the Egyptians have told me, while adding some things from my own observation." At the second (2.147) he says: "This, then, is what the Egyptians themselves say; I will now proceed to relate what both other people and the Egyptians, agreeing with them, say about what happened in the country, while adding some things from my own observation." This last division marks the start of the Saite dynasty (XXVI) in 663 BC, some two hundred years before Herodotus' time; the "other people" are Ionians and Carians who, Herodotus says a few pages later (2.154), helped the first Saite king, Psammetichus, gain the throne and were rewarded with permission to settle in the country. Furthermore, Psammetichus had some Egyptian boys taught Greek, which was the beginning of the Egyptian class of interpreters: "After this settlement in Egypt the Greeks had regular contact with them and thus, from the time of King Psammetichus on, we have accurate knowledge of all events in Egypt." The divisions are therefore based not on types of subject matter but on sources of information and their worth: eyes, ears, inference and inquiry. Particularly significant is the emphasis on more recent events and on the possibility of cross-checking one account with another: accuracy increased dramatically when both can be brought into play. And, in fact, Herodotus in the first and second parts accepts much of what the Egyptians told him with little demur. But in the last section he is at times quite critical of what the Egyptians say, and of their motives for saying it (e.g. 3.2, 16).

Yet overall Herodotus presents an uneven picture of what he thought his role as an inquirer should be. At times he declares forthrightly what he thinks about matters that are in dispute or possibly unpopular, such as the decisive (in his eyes) role that Athens played in defeating Persia (7.139). Occasionally he will go into great detail, as when he analyzes three theories advanced by "some Greeks who want to be known for their cleverness" to explain the flooding of the Nile. He rejects their theories (including the correct one that snow is the cause: how could there be snow in an area that became hotter the further south one went?). At the end he gives his own quite ingenious view (2.20–27). In fact, in his long digression on Egypt he is more combative than elsewhere in the *Histories*: against Hecataeus, against Homer, against unnamed Ionians, against silly Greeks in general. He heaps scorn particularly on those who claim that Ocean is a river that encircles the earth and that the Nile originates from it: the claim, he says, cannot be verified and is probably the invention of Homer or some other early poet (2.23).

But with equal frequency he simply reports what he has heard without passing judgment, even on matters that seem quite absurd, such as gold-digging ants bigger than foxes, some specimens of which, he reports, were in the Persian king's private zoo (3.102). He believes it an important part of his job to report what people say about themselves, but not regularly to subject it to critical analysis: "I am bound to report what is told to me, but I am by no means bound to believe it, and this may be taken to apply to my work as a whole" (7.152; cf. 2.123, 4.195).

Herodotus thus reports the various traditions as he heard them. Recent work on travellers in other periods who reported on what they encountered in strange lands provides fascinating analogies for the sort of cultural bias we see in Herodotus; a particularly telling example is the description by Europeans of what they found or thought they had found in the New World. Recent work on oral tradition in general, especially in Africa, has produced valuable insights on how native traditions are fashioned: their recollections reflect not what necessarily happened but what an individual or group wants to remember. Furthermore, these traditions are refashioned over time to suit the preferences of a changing society. Nor does remembrance that is passed down orally last much beyond three generations, or 125 years.

Herodotus sometimes reflects the bias of his sources, and sometimes himself favors the places he lived in or visited, such as the island of Samos, Athens and Egypt. For Samos he shows much knowledge and affection (3.39–60), although rather neutrally mentioning several examples of Samian naval pirateering (3.47). As for Egypt, he clearly was impressed by the antiquity of the country, especially its long history, and with the many marvels that were to be found there. When he found certain Greek practices to be similar to those of the Egyptians, it must invariably mean, he believes, that the Greeks borrowed from the Egyptians, for they were a much older people and had kept records going back thousands of years (e.g. 2.49–58, 77–82, 145). Egypt looms large in Herodotus' thinking as a historian (on which more below): the country bowled him over, so to speak. As for Athens, he is outspoken in his praise of the city as the bastion of freedom and proof of the success that freedom brings (5.78). Some of his information appears to have come from the noble Alcmaeonid family, to which Pericles' mother belonged (he gives Pericles' pedigree at 6.131). He presents a defense of the family against charges of collaboration with Persia and of sympathy to the tyranny of the Pisistratids in the sixth century. He asserts that this tyrant-hating family was in exile during the entire period when Pisistratus and his son Hippias were in control in Athens (6.123). Yet a surviving inscription shows that one of its most prominent members, Cleisthenes, was chief archon under Hippias: Herodotus' Alcmaeonid informants were disingenuous indeed. Yet Herodotus does not hesitate to give information that puts the family in a discreditable light. For example, he describes the ridiculous figure cut by Alcmaeon, founder of the family's great wealth, as he staggered from the treasury of King Croesus, gold dust stuffed in his clothes, boots, hair and mouth, "looking like anything but a man" (6.125). Alcmaeonid dislike of Themistocles appears to be behind the charges of bribery and greed attributed to the hero of Salamis (e.g. 8.5, 112). Moreover, the enemies and friends that Athens made in the course of acquiring her empire from 479 to 431 BC are reflected in his accounts of many places in the *Histories*. Corinth is a prime example, for she was Sparta's major ally and the power that did most to urge Sparta to stand up to Athens, thereby precipitating the Peloponnesian War. Nevertheless, Herodotus frankly reveals the bias of his Athenian sources in a passage at 8.94: at the Battle of Salamis, the Athenians said, the Corinthians panicked and sailed off, rejoining the main fleet after the battle had been won: "Such is the story the Athenians tell, but the Corinthians disagree, maintaining that they were in the forefront of the fighting— and the rest of Greece bears witness to what they say" (8.94).

One of Herodotus' greatest preoccupations is with accomplishments that surprise, astonish and amaze (*thômata*). He likes to bring out his tape measure to determine the dimensions of vast constructions like the pyramids and other tombs (e.g. 1.93, 2.123–127), and he wants to know the weight, size and materials of the objects he sees (e.g. 1.50–52). He justifies his lengthy account of Samian history because the island boasts three of the greatest engineering feats in the Greek world (3.60): first, a tunnel through a mountain nearly a mile long, eight feet in height and width, and he names the engineer: Eupalinus, son of Naustrophus; second, a harbor created by a breakwater twenty fathoms in depth and a quarter mile in length; third, the largest temple in the Greek world, whose architect was Rhoecus, son of Phileus: "It is because of these works that I have given a rather full account of Samian history," he concludes. He gives a similar explanation to justify his huge digression on Egypt (2.35): "I intend to to give a lengthy account (*logos*) of Egypt because it has the greatest number of marvels and offers more monuments that beggar description (*logos*!) than any other country. And this is why I will say rather a lot about it." There is, then, a significant element in Herodotus that might be labelled "believe-it-or-not." This of course adds much interest and charm to his narrative; no doubt these marvels are included partly because Herodotus is fascinated with them for their own sake.

But the matter goes deeper. Marvels or *thômata* include not only what man has built but what he has done: history, in other words. Herodotus in fact gives far more emphasis to the great and astounding achievements of his historical characters than to physical objects that they may have created: for example, Cyrus' defeat of Croesus and his capture of Babylon, or Darius' invasion of Scythia and his narrow escape when retreating back across the Danube. Unforgettable is the picture of Xerxes as he looks down from his throne on the bay of Salamis: before his eyes his huge armada is destroyed by a much smaller Greek force (8.66 ff.). Reason and calculation say he should prevail. Most Greeks thought he would prevail. Even the Delphic oracle was inclined to think so. But he lost: the Battle of Salamis is one of the *Histories'* greatest *thômata*, although he gives pride of place to the Battle of Plataea: "the finest victory of all those we know of" (9.64).

There is another important reason for Herodotus' interest in the amazing and the astonishing. As he stresses strongly in the proem, his chief purpose in writing is "so that man's past may not fade into oblivion over time nor the great and amazing deeds displayed by both Greeks and barbarians be without renown." In other words, his *Histories* are to constitute a memorial to greatness, an attempt to prevent the lapse of time from inexorably erasing the memory of things. The metaphor in the first clause suggests a stone inscription whose letters fade with weathering; in the second the word for "without renown," *aklea*, has strong Homeric overtones. Homer's heroes are greatly concerned about their glory (*kleos*) going unrecognized or unappreciated. Homer's poems, like Herodotus' *Histories*, thus fulfill the same purpose: they commemorate greatness, and through their own high qualities they ensure that men's deeds will live in the minds of future generations. And they were right. It became a commonplace in antiquity to recognize that without literature the most memorable individuals and accomplishments would fade to nothingness: if Homer had not written about Achilles, men would not know of him—only a grave tumulus on the plain of Troy would survive, and no one would be able to put a name even to that. Thus Herodotus is at great pains to name those whose deeds deserve commemoration, such as the engineer of the Samian tunnel and the architect of the island's great temple. At the conclusion of major battles he is concerned to name those who gave outstanding service, both cities and individuals, and, as the proem says, to highlight both barbarian and Greek achievements equally. The Battle of Thermopylae is an illustration (7.224–228). At the start of his review he says (7.224):

Leonidas also fell in the struggle, having shown himself the finest fighter, and many other Spartiates with him worth naming, whose names I have made myself acquainted with because they were worthy men; I have also become acquainted with the names of all three hundred who fell.

He then specifies the most outstanding of these Spartiate fighters (but forebears to name all three hundred). Those Persians who fought with the greatest distinction are also listed.

Herodotus' penchant for including bizarre information that astonishes and surprises made him vulnerable to much criticism both in antiquity and in modern times. For example, Ctesias, a Greek physician at the Persian court in the generation after Herodotus, wrote his own accounts of India and Persia, in which he derided Herodotus for his ignorance and exaggerations. What readers in antiquity expected in histories were realism and verisimilitude. Compare, for example, the two versions, mentioned in the last chapter, of the slaying of Geryon by Heracles as given by Dionysius of Halicarnassus, one "mythical" the other "historical." Cicero (*On the Laws* 1.5) in the same breath characterizes Herodotus as the father of history and the purveyor of "countless tall tales."

In modern times Herodotus has fared little better at the hands of some critics, especially those toward the end of the nineteenth century. Father of History was a misnomer, they said: Father of Lies is closer to the mark. One passage sometimes singled out to illustrate this contention comes at 3.111–113 in a discussion of the wonders of Arabia. Herodotus relates three of them in rapid succession. The first is about cinnamon: the sticks are found only in the nests that certain large birds build on narrow ledges high on inaccessible cliffs. To get the cinnamon, natives cut up bodies of dead animals; the birds fly down, pick up the pieces and return to their nests, which break under the added weight and fall to the ground. The natives then rush out to gather the cinnamon sticks. Such is the source of cinnamon, Herodotus says. The second concerns the source of ledanon, a sweet-smelling substance that was used to make the finest ancient perfumes. Billy goats were set to grazing among the ledanon bushes, and from their beards the ledanon was combed out. Hence the sweetest of substances was gathered from the beards of the smelliest of animals. The third describes sheep whose tails are so large that they become sore and infected from dragging on the ground. So the shepherds make miniature wheeled carts for each sheep to pull, laying the tail on the cart. At first sight these stories do seem far-fetched; but in the course of the early part of this century two of them were discovered to be true (the goats and the sheep). The lesson is clear: condemning Herodotean tales out of hand because they do not seem likely may be more an indication of the parochial viewpoint of critics than of Herodotean naivety. In the course of his travels Herodotus saw and heard of so many marvels that he was reluctant simply to dismiss them out of hand. A commendable broadmindedness was the result, which some of his critics, ancient and modern, have not proved to possess themselves. Even today Herodotus is subject to wholesale dismissal: the sources he cites are almost wholly fictitious, some claim; others affirm he did not visit many of the places he says he did, but copied from Hecataeus, who *did* visit the places he wrote about.

One must admit that there are quite a few errors in Herodotus on matters that he states or implies he saw firsthand and that he attributes an uncomfortable number of Greek myths and ideas to foreign sources; to give a satisfactory explanation of some of these difficulties is not easy. But wholesale rejection of the information he gives is unwarranted. His errors are counterbalanced by a great many statements that are correct, which a storyteller in the tradition of the *Arabian Nights* would scarcely have bothered to get right. His account of such a technical matter as mummification has been declared by Egyptologists to be tolerably accurate (2.86–88). On a more strictly historical matter, of the seven Persian conspirators who plotted against the false Smerdis in 521 BC, he correctly names six of them, while the seventh is close to the correct form (and was, in any case, a genuine Persian name, for we find it on a Persian inscription as the name of Darius' quiver-bearer). As a final instance, it is instructive to note that the one feature of the story of the three-year circumnavigation of Africa by the Phoenicians that excites his distrust is the one that (for us) proves it true: namely, as the ship was sailing from east to west around the Cape of Good Hope, the sun appeared on the sailors' right (4.42).

In a remarkable passage at 2.31–34 Herodotus discusses the vexed question of the source of the Nile. Beyond Egypt, he reports, one could follow its course for a distance that took four months to traverse; at that point the river was flowing from west to east; beyond it no one knew anything. In Cyrene on the African coast west of Egypt (modern Benghazi in Libya), some people told him a story they heard from Etearchus, king of the Ammonians, who in turn heard it from some

Nasamonians who inhabited an area near his kingdom. Certain Nasamonian youths decided on a dare to explore the Sahara further than anyone had ever gone. Taking plenty of food and water, they trekked through the desert until they came to a settlement of black pygmies situated on a great river with crocodiles in it. The river flowed from west to east.

> Now Etearchus conjectured that the river flowing by was also the Nile, and reason (*logos*) certainly supports this view. For the Nile flows from Africa and cuts through the middle of it. And it is my conjecture, judging the unknown from the known, that it has its origin the same distance from its mouth as does the Danube. For the Danube River, beginning among the Celts and the town of Pyrene, cuts through the middle of Europe. . . . The Danube ends by flowing into the Black Sea, having run the length of Europe, where the Milesian colonists settled the town of Istria. The Danube, since it flows through inhabited country, is known by many people, but no one is able to speak about the source of the Nile because the part of Africa through which it flows is an uninhabited desert. That is what I have to report about its course, having gone as far as I was able to go in my inquiries (*historeô*). It enters Egypt from the country beyond. Now Egypt is situated just about opposite the mountains of Cilicia. From there to Sinope on the Black Sea the journey is one of five days for a man travelling light. And Sinope is opposite the mouth of the Danube. Therefore I think the Nile, flowing through the whole of Africa, is equal in length to the Danube.
>
> (2.33–34)

If the story of the crossing of the Sahara has some basis, as it seems to have, the river the Nasamonians encountered was probably the Niger. But its flow from west to east and the fact that crocodiles lived in it caused Etearchus to identify it as the Nile, "and reason certainly supports this view," adds Herodotus. He then contributes his own conjecture, based on the analogy of the course of the Danube. Clearly he finds it reasonable that geography should exhibit balance and symmetry: both the Nile and the Danube would then cut through the center of their respective continents, both would begin and end at approximately the same longitudes (the mouth of the Nile being aligned with the Cilician mountains, Sinope and the mouth of the Danube). Clearly Herodotus' knowledge of the geography of the far west is shaky (cf. 3.115–116): the Pyrenees have become a town, and

29

just where he would place the Rhone, if he knew of it, in relation to the Danube is unclear (at 4.49 the Alps are identified as a northward-flowing river tributary to the Danube).

This tale illustrates forcibly how prone Herodotus was to see physical features such as geography in terms of balance and order. Clearly the view of the world as exhibiting and exemplifying *kosmos* is behind Herodotus' thinking in this passage. The influence, however, was, as far as we can judge, indirect. Herodotus' beliefs here and elsewhere on balance and order reflect a commonly held view of the world; they do not necessarily derive from specific thinkers or theories.

Herodotus' belief in *kosmos* is evident in many other places. The world is envisioned as something like a flat disc, with Greece roughly in the center. In India at its eastern edge the sun as it rises over the rim is closest to that country; hence the mornings are very hot, the rest of the day cooling off steadily as the sun moves away to the west (3.104: presumably the far west would correspondingly be hottest at the end of the day). The further north one goes, the colder it becomes, and the further south the hotter. The people living furthest to the north were said to be the Hyperboreans, or those living beyond Boreas, the north wind. "If Hyperboreans exist," Herodotus says, "there must also be Hypernotions:" that is, those dwelling beyond the south wind, Notos (4.36). Furthermore, while the ends of the earth produce the finest things in size, scarcity and value, Greece, lying in the middle, has the finest climate, a blend of the extremes one finds at the edges of the world (3.106).

However, Herodotus' clearest and most far-reaching example of balance and antithesis is his contrast between the two countries he describes most fully, Egypt and Scythia. They are mirror opposites of one another in all sorts of ways, each exemplifying extremes of "otherness" in relation to Greece in between. One is the country of heat in the south, the other of cold in the north; one of no rain, the other of summer rain (whereas in the Mediterranean winter is generally the rainy season). Egypt is dominated by a single river that has no tributaries, flows from south to north (unlike other rivers) in its Egyptian part and floods in early summer when others are drying up. Scythia is divided by a great many large rivers with numerous tributaries. The Nile holds Egypt together and defines it; Scythia's rivers split the country into many parts, creating barriers to travel and invasion. Yet paradoxically the creation of man-made canals make travel in Egypt by wagon or horses impossible, whereas these are the means the Scythians use to move around their country. Egypt used to

30

be mostly marshland; when it was drained and a canal system begun, the greater part of the country's usable land was created. Moreover, this land is divided into equal lots; geometry was invented to subserve the need for surveying. Egypt is therefore in large part an artificial, man-made creation. But Scythia exists in its natural state, and nothing has been done to alter it; there was, in fact, a long period when it lay unpopulated, for the Scythians believe themselves to be the youngest people on earth.

The cultures of the two countries are also opposed to one another. The Egyptians are fixed cultivators and have many cities; the Scythians are nomads and have none. The Egyptian kings build great memorials to hold their bodies; the burial grounds of the Scythian kings cannot be located by those coming from outside. Egypt has more wonders than any other nation; Scythia's rivers constitute its sole wonder, save for a footprint of Heracles in a rock (4.82). The Egyptians are the great inventors and discoverers: the solar year, the names of the twelve gods and so forth; the Scythians have invented only a single thing, the great art of not being conquered. In fact, there is but one entrance into Egypt, but once that entrance is breached, the country may be conquered easily; Scythia cannot be captured because it exists in no definable place or places. It may be easy to invade Scythia, but once you are there you paradoxically cannot find it.

Finally, the histories of the two places are also antithetical. The Scythians, who claim to be the youngest nation on earth, have no history to speak of, save for a few foundation legends. The Egyptians claim to be the oldest nation (although an experiment showed them to be second oldest: 2.2). They have records reaching back many thousands of years, from Min the first king to the present: to be precise, 341 generations spanning 11,000 years (2.142). In short (2.77), "those of the Egyptians who live in the cultivated part of the country are, of the people I have had experience of, the most knowledgeable of all men in memory [of the past]." The history of Egypt in more recent times had been one of conquest by outsiders, but Scythia had never succumbed. In terms of the history with which Herodotus is concerned, Cambyses' conquest of Egypt and Darius' failed expedition against the Scythians are the events most prominently featured between Cyrus' establishment of the Persian Empire and the Ionian Revolt.

Balance and symmetry extend from the world of geography, nations and customs to the world of nature (3.108). "Somehow the fore-thought of god, being wise, as it certainly seems to be, has brought it

31

about that all creatures timid and edible produce many offspring, so that when eaten some survive, but whatever are savage and predatory have few progeny." Herodotus then proceeds to illustrate this idea by reviewing fertility among hares, lions, adders and flying snakes (his views of these biological matters range from the uninformed to the fantastic).

Herodotus' picture of the physical world and of nature is thus dominated by symmetry, antithesis and balance. But it should be emphasized that although his tendency to view things in this fashion is strong, it is only a tendency: it is not invariable or procrustean. For example, he rejects the idea of a circumambient Ocean, although that would fit the idea of *kosmos* nicely. Nor does he name Delphi, which influenced him greatly, or any other place in the Greek world the "navel of the earth," although this was claimed for Delphi and some other shrines. Again, this would have fitted well with his general view. Nor are the continents and seas of the same or complementary size and shape. One could, in fact, list a whole series of inconcinnities and irregularities that do not fit with the notion of a world of balance and antithesis: Egypt, it turned out, was not the oldest country, but the second oldest; certain parts of Scythia were in fact under cultivation by settled inhabitants, and so forth. Herodotus' willingness to accept and mention in his *Histories* such irregularities was doubtless the result of his own inquiries: the more he travelled in the world, the more he became aware of its variety and complexity. *Kosmos* was therefore a general characteristic, something one might expect to find but sometimes did not. When evidence failed to fit in with it, Herodotus did not force it into a preconceived mold, ignore it or explain it away.

In one area he was forcibly struck by the differences among the peoples he visited: their customs and laws (*nomoi*, singular *nomos*). An almost bewildering variety of *nomoi* were to be found, so much so that at times the customs of some people seemed utterly at variance with those in use elsewhere. Egypt is a striking instance: at 2.35–36 he lists some eighteen oppositions, from sex roles to diet to bathroom habits. Nowhere is his relativism shown more clearly than in the field of religion. On the one hand, the same gods rule the world everywhere, but man's apprehension of them takes on an astonishing variety of forms in almost every aspect—names, appearance and worship. Moreover, some peoples know of relatively few gods: mankind in general comes to know about the gods from one another. Greece, for example, learned of most of her gods from Egypt, the far older civilization (2.4); on the other hand, there were Greek deities, such

32

as Poseidon and the Dioscuri, whom the Egyptians did not worship (2.43, 53). The practice of religion, in short, is a historically determined phenomenon. Herodotus is fond of recording the many odd and strange forms of worship that he encountered (odd and strange, that is, to a Greek). A few of them he seems to imply are backward or barbaric (e.g. human sacrifice, 4.62), but his stated position is this (2.3): "I think all men have an equal understanding of these [religious] matters." Rarely does he express disapproval of a custom (temple prostitution among the Babylonians is one, 1.199).

His travels instilled in him a great tolerance for the customs of others as well as a positive appreciation of their merits; later in antiquity he was criticized as a "barbarian lover." The most famous passage on the place of *nomos* in the world comes at 3.38:

> It is crystal clear to me that King Cambyses went completely out of his mind. Otherwise he would not have ventured to mock the sacred rites and customs [of the Egyptians]. For if any man whosoever were asked to select the best customs out of all that exist, upon examination each would choose his own. Every man thinks his own customs to be much the best. So it is not likely that anyone but a madman would laugh at such things. That all men think this way about the question of *nomoi* can be established by a great many proofs, one of them being this: during his reign Darius asked some Greeks who happened to be present how much money they would take to eat the dead bodies of their fathers; they said they would not do it for anything. In the presence of the Greeks, who were told through interpreters what was said, Darius then asked some Indians, known as Callatiae and who ate their parents, how much money they would take to cremate the dead bodies of their fathers; they gave a shriek and begged him not to mention such a sinful thing. This then is the way men think about *nomos*, and Pindar seems to me to have rightly called it "king of all."

Relativism thus looms large in Herodotus' eyes. Men and nations are perforce culture-bound: they act and think in accordance with their traditions and upbringing.

In the confrontation between Greece and Persia that forms the climax of the *Histories* the clash is not solely or even primarily military. More fundamental and more significant is the cultural clash, involving matters of values, priorities and each side's understanding of the other, or lack of it.

The Persians are the products of an oriental monarchy. The king's power is absolute: each subject is his slave. All look to him for safety and sustenance, and regard whatever benefits they enjoy, including their lives, as in his gift. Hence Xerxes believes his subjects will not on their own act bravely or honorably: he is the motivating force behind what they do. They must be whipped into battle, for example (e.g. Thermopylae, 7.223), and in the fighting itself each man will do his best "out of fear, believing that the king's eyes will be upon him" (Salamis, 8.86). Xerxes' power leads him to say and do things unthinkable for a Greek, but that come quite naturally to him. The wealthy Lydian Pythius is an example: after being the conspicuous recipient of Xerxes' favor he ventured to ask that instead of all five of his sons accompanying the king to Greece the youngest be allowed to stay behind with himself. This enraged the monarch: how dare one of his slaves suggest such a thing when he himself was marching to Greece? He ordered the youngest son be cut in two and the army to march out between the halves fixed on each side of the road (7.39). Xerxes' whipping, cursing and branding of the Hellespont for having destroyed his bridge from Asia to Europe is another example of his megalomania (7.34), as is the story of the magnificent plane tree he came across during his march. Taken with the tree's beauty, Xerxes had it decorated with gold ornaments and assigned one of his elite bodyguards to watch over it (7.31). Tree and guard dwindle into the distance as king and army continue on their way.

During the march to Greece the exiled Spartan king Demaratus accompanied Xerxes as an advisor. Herodotus features two conversations between them in order to illustrate the utterly different mind-sets of the Greeks and the Persians. The first comes after Xerxes has reviewed all of his naval and land forces after crossing the Hellespont into Europe (7.101–104). Will the Greeks dare to confront such a mighty army as this? Demaratus assures him that they will, especially his fellow Spartiates. If there should be only a thousand of them, they would still take the field against him. This is Xerxes' reply:

> Come now! Consider the likelihood of such a thing. How could a thousand, or ten thousand, or fifty thousand—all being free and not under the control of one man—stand up against an army like this? If there were fifty thousand we would still outnumber them by more than a thousand to one. If they were under the control of one man, as in our system, possibly they might out of fear of him prove better fighters than they normally would be

and might attack when under the whips, even though outnumbered. But since they are completely free to do as they
please, they would do neither of these things.

This is part of Demaratus' reply:

> These men indeed are free, but they are not completely free. For
> *nomos* is their master, and they fear it much more than your
> subjects do you. For they do what *nomos* commands, and this
> command is always the same: not to flee the enemy, however
> many they may be, but to stay in position and to win or die.

Xerxes said nothing in reply, Herodotus reports, but burst out
laughing. What Demaratus said made no sense.

The second conversation occurs as the Battle of Thermopylae is
about to begin. Xerxes sends a scout to reconnoiter the pass (7.208–
209). The spy finds a small number of Spartiates there, who took no
notice of him, but continued to exercise and comb their hair, as they
had been doing. Xerxes could not believe that these men were really
preparing to fight: it was laughable. So he sent for Demaratus, who
assured him that such was the case: it was the custom (*nomos*) of the
Spartiates to comb their hair before risking their lives in battle. Once
again Xerxes was not persuaded: the idea was incomprehensible.

The clash between East and West thus takes on a deeper meaning
than either its ostensible cause—punishment of Athens and Eretria—
or the unfolding of its military operations would suggest. More
fundamental by far is the cultural ethos of the two antagonists:
autocracy versus freedom. Herodotus makes it plain where he stands.
Despotism inhibits the open expression of views. Subjects tend to say
and do what they think the autocrat wants. Autocracy thus carries
within itself the seeds of its own undoing, for many will be reluctant to
tell the monarch what they really think. Moreover, autocracy is a huge
monolith whose very size and rigidity comprise another major weakness. Freedom, on the other hand, while fostering competition, rivalry
and disunity within its ranks, paradoxically generates strength
through flexibility and the energy that competition promotes.
Herodotus cites Athens as the prime example (5.78). Under the tyranny
of the Pisistratids they were no better fighters than their neighbors, but
when the tyrants were driven out they proved far the best: "Clearly the
reason is that when they were subjects they deliberately played the
coward, since they were acting in the interests of a master, but when
they became free each man acted in his own interest."

3

FATHER OF HISTORY

The Roman statesman Cicero was the first of whom we know to call Herodotus Father of History (*On the Laws* 1.5). No one in antiquity seems to have disputed his primacy, although a few in modern times have thought Hecataeus deserving of the title. Yet scarcely any of Hecataeus' fragments suggest he discussed the history of either Greece or foreign peoples (although direct speech is attested: *FGrH* 1T20); his interests were in myth, genealogy, geography and ethnography. Herodotus claims the title by default. Yet how deserving was he? How good an historian was the founder of the genre?

In the fifth century BC the majority of people considered myth and legend as much a part of their history as recent events. But the invention of history proper depended on making a marked distinction between the two. This Herodotus did, and upon it rests one of the main supports for his title Father of History. We have already noted the importance he attached to testing the veracity of what was told him by cross-checking among two or more different sources. This might, of course, concern matters far back in time, such as the antiquity of the cult of Heracles, discussed in the last chapter. But since opportunities to cross-check with those knowledgeable about such ancient subjects are scarce (the Egyptians were especially useful here: see below), he places far more emphasis on events closer in time, when the remembrance of things is fresher and widespread. The more recent history of Egypt (from 663 BC on) is one example, when Carian and Greek mercenaries were allowed to establish a permanent settlement in the country: from that point on one could check the account given by the Egyptians with what these settlers, who knew the country firsthand, had to say (2.147, 154).

But the question goes deeper and has wider ramifications. In a remarkable passage that comes at the point when he is making precisely the transition to more recent Egyptian history (2.141–146), Herodotus speaks of the great antiquity of the country; the priests of Zeus (=Amun) in Thebes assured him that 341 generations of both pharaohs and priests of Hephaestus (=Ptah) separated the first king Min from the start of the Saite dynasty in 663 BC. Reckoning three generations as a hundred years, Herodotus arrives at a total of 11,340 years. During all this time, the priests affirmed, no god had ever appeared in Egypt in mortal form. Yet, says Herodotus,

> When Hecataeus, the *logopoios*, was in Thebes and gave his genealogy, he traced his ancestry back to a god in the sixteenth generation; what is more, the priests of Zeus did to him what they did to me, although I did not give my genealogy. Leading the way into a large interior room, they counted off as many wooden statues as I have mentioned [i.e. 341]. . . . When Hecataeus gave his genealogy going back to a god in the sixteenth generation they refuted his pedigree on the basis of the number, refusing to accept from him that a man was born to a god. They refuted it by saying that each of the statues represented a *piromis* born of a *piromis*, pointing out 345 of the statues, nor did they connect any of them either to a god or a hero (*piromis* is the Egyptian word for "gentleman").
>
> (2.143)

Clearly the additional four generations represent the period between the beginning of the Saite dynasty in 663 and Hecataeus' visit to Egypt around 500 BC.

Herodotus then launches into a discussion of chronology. The Greeks reckon Dionysus, Heracles and Pan the youngest of the gods; Greek genealogy would place the birth of Dionysus 1,600 years in the past, that of Heracles 900 years and that of Pan 800 years (the last occurring *after* the events of the Trojan War, Herodotus notes). The Egyptians, on the other hand, reckon Pan (=Min) as a member of the oldest order of gods, Heracles (=Shu or Khonsu) among the next oldest and Dionysus (=Osiris) among the gods born in the generation after Heracles. Yet even Dionysus, the youngest of the three, was born fifteen thousand years ago! "The Egyptians say that they have exact knowledge of these matters, continually calculating and continually recording the years" (2.145). Hence, when a people like the Egyptians possess such ancient records, they earned in Herodotus' eyes the right to be believed. Furthermore, if no gods had appeared on earth in Egypt for over eleven thousand years, they could scarcely have appeared anywhere else either, for it is childish to suppose that Greece experienced continual theophanies and Egypt none in the same period of time.

The consequences of these revelations for Herodotus' view of early Greek history were profound. For if the gods had not appeared on earth and had not interfered directly in man's activities, what Homer said must be partly false. And the genealogies of Greek families, like that of Hecataeus (and probably his own), must be partly false as well. A great blow was thus struck at one of the props of early Greek history: the descent of its leading families. The Greeks are therefore far inferior to the Egyptians in their knowledge of the past. In fact, the Greeks learned of the existence of most of their gods from Egypt "yesterday or the day before, so to speak" (2.53).

In this same passage on the antiquity of the gods, Herodotus then speculates (2.146) on how the Greeks could have mistakenly believed Pan, Heracles and Dionysus to be recent divinities. The reason must be that the Greeks came to know of them later than the other gods and that they traced their genealogies from the moment they learned of them; it may also be, he speculates, that originally Dionysus and Pan were humans who bore the names of previously existing gods but later somehow became confused with the gods themselves (Heracles being born a mortal in any case).

His reasoning about why the Greeks came to have erroneous views about the antiquity of Heracles, Dionysus and Pan deserves closer scrutiny. Nowadays we tend to dismiss most myths and legends as prima facie fabricated out of whole cloth: they may tell us much about the culture and values of the people in later years who believed in them, but they do not of themselves give reliable information about the period in which they were purportedly set. Possibly there was a Trojan War of sorts, for example, but beyond even this debatable proposition one cannot go. When we see Greeks rationalizing their myths, therefore, we tend to interpret this as an attempt to "save" the stories by eliminating the miraculous, impossible and improbable elements. But Herodotus and his fellow Greeks did not view these efforts as ones of salvage. Rather, from the outset they took a positive viewpoint: there must be some truth to these stories because something does not come from nothing. They therefore have a basis in fact, and one should try to recover as much of that "fact" as one can. In their eyes to dismiss myth and legend out of hand as wholesale inventions was to throw the baby out with the bathwater (and after Sir Arthur Evans at the start of this century found a labyrinthine palace in Crete where bull worship was practiced, many began to think there might be something in this approach: for here was evidence for the legends of both Minos and Theseus). In the passage discussed above Herodotus accepts both that gods had not assumed human shape on earth for over eleven thousand years, as the Egyptians claim, and that the erroneous Greek belief that Heracles, Dionysus and Pan were the youngest of the gods had a factual explanation as well.

Not only did Hecataeus' contretemps with the Egyptian priests strike a blow against the Greek genealogical approach to early times, but against history of the type that Homer and other poets told. Herodotus' detailed discussion of Helen shows this clearly (2.112–120). The Egyptians claimed to have knowledge of her throughout the Trojan conflict. After Alexander (=Paris) had abducted her from her husband Menelaus in Sparta, the two were headed for Troy when bad weather blew their ship off course to Egypt. After various misadventures on the part of Alexander, King Proteus decided to let him go but to detain Helen and the property Alexander had stolen from Menelaus. The sources of the information are specified: priests at Memphis reported what they heard from the priests of the temple of Hephaestus at the Canopic mouth of the Nile and from the guard of the Canopic mouth (he is named: Thonis), as well as what they directly learned during Helen's stay at the court of King Proteus in Memphis. After the fall of Troy Menelaus appeared in Egypt to pick up Helen on his return voyage to Sparta; he spoke directly to the priests about what had transpired during the ten-year siege. After Menelaus' escape from their country the Egyptians could not say what happened to him next: "They affirm that they know of some of these facts from inquiry (*historeô*), while having exact knowledge of the events that occurred in their own country" (2.119).

Homer, then, was wrong to say that Helen was in Troy during the ten-year siege. Yet Herodotus believes that Homer knew the real facts, and quotes several passages from the *Iliad* and *Odyssey* that in his eyes support this belief. Why, then, did Homer choose not to narrate the true version? Because, says Herodotus, "it was not as appealing for epic poetry as the one he used." The basic meaning of the word for "appealing," *euprepês*, is "having an attractive appearance." The standards, then, for epic poetry are not those by which Herodotus operates in the new genre of history: one can expect in Homer and other poets versions that are false, even when the poet knows the truth. Hesiod, for example, freely admitted that the Muses inspired him with false tales similar to true ones (*Theogony* 27). Not surprisingly, then, Herodotus finds other examples where poets and history part company. One idea, mentioned before, is that the world was encircled by a river called Ocean; this is "an invention by Homer or some other of the early poets and brought over into poetry" (2.23). When Herodotus says that some accepted this idea in explaining the flooding of the Nile, he describes it as a "myth" (*muthos*), which he characterizes as "unintelligent" and "incapable of proof" (2.21, 23). The unnamed person under attack was Hecataeus, as we can see from one of his fragments (*FGrH* 1F302c); from another (*FGrH* 1F18a) we learn Hecataeus' explanation of how the ship *Argo* returned to the Mediterranean: it sailed down the Nile from Ocean beyond. Hecataeus by implication, then, is tarred with the same brush as is Homer: he uncritically accepted a poetic invention for which empirical evidence provides no proof. Herodotus also characterizes the Eridanus River in the far west of Europe as another poetic invention (3.115).

It is instructive to pursue Herodotus' reasoning in the matter of Helen (2.120). He says he is inclined to believe the Egyptian version that Helen was in their country during the Trojan War because King Priam would never have allowed his people to suffer such great losses over so many years simply to let Alexander enjoy Helen's company (he was not even the heir apparent, Herodotus notes). Priam himself lost two or more sons in each of the battles that were fought ("if one is to trust the epic poets," he adds); why, even if Helen had been his own consort he would have handed her back in order to avoid the disasters piling up on himself and his city. So Helen was not in Troy, and when the Greeks kept asking for her return and that of the stolen property, the Trojans kept saying they did not have them. But then, Herodotus asks, why over the course of ten years were the Greeks so pig-headed as not eventually to see that what the Trojans said was true? Divine punishment is Herodotus' answer for this impasse that appears to have no rational explanation on the human level: the gods blinded the Greeks to the truth in order to punish Troy for Alexander's violation of the sacred obligations of guest and host.

Herodotus may give us on occasion myths and legends of bygone eras, such as the delightful tales of Rhampsinitus and the thieves from early Egyptian history (2.121) or how the Amazons learned about sex (4.110–117). But his overwhelming concentration is upon recent history, especially that of the last hundred years, from the founding of the Persian Empire by Cyrus ca. 560 BC. This period answers pretty much to what students of oral history tell us is the maximum that one can expect oral traditions reliably to survive: three generations or approximately one hundred years, if not a bit more.

The start of the *Histories* stresses the point emphatically. After the proem Herodotus reviews four myths that he claims certain "knowledgeable Persians" cite to fix responsibility for the clash between East and West (1–5: the attribution of these rationalized versions of well-known Greek myths to Persians is puzzling, since it seems improbable that Persians would know of or care about such Greek stories). The first concerns the kidnapping of Io, princess of Argos in Greece, by Phoenician sailors, who took her to Egypt (Io is not transformed into a heifer in this version; she gets pregnant by the ship captain and sails off with him to escape the shame of eventual detection). Some Greeks then retaliated by kidnapping Europa, Princess of Tyre in Phoenicia (Europa leaves not on the back of a bull but in a Cretan boat). Then came Medea's turn, Princess of Colchis at the eastern end of the Black Sea; when her father demanded reparation and the return of his daughter, the Greeks refused, not having received, they said, satisfaction for the abduction of Io. Finally, Alexander of Troy kidnapped Helen; Greek demands for satisfaction were rebuffed by the Trojans, who cited Medea's abduction. But the Greeks went further and did something hitherto unprecedented: they actually went to war over the last of these kidnapped ladies. This the knowledgeable Persians thought silly, Herodotus reports, since in their view women are not abducted unless they wish to be. The Greeks were therefore the first to make a military response, according to the Persians: "From this point on they have never ceased to consider the Greeks as hostile to them. For the Persians claim Asia and the barbarian peoples living there as within their domain, and view Europe and the Greeks as separate" (1.4).

In a grand gesture Herodotus then sweeps aside these mythical fables. He will not bother "to say whether these events happened in this or some other way, but I will name the man *I* know to have first wronged the Greeks, . . . Croesus of Lydia" (1.5–6). The contrast could scarcely be more pointed. Whatever Herodotus' motives for beginning his *Histories* with these abduction myths and attributing them to "knowledgeable Persians," the chief one was to make a sharp distinction between then and now, between unsubstantiated stories and "what *I* know." And, in fact, the phrase "the first of whom I (or we) know" runs like a leitmotif throughout the *Histories*, appearing more than thirty times. Often it is an emphatic marker that differentiates recent history from the distant past. For example, Gyges of Lydia was

41

"the first barbarian of whom we know to send dedications to Delphi after Midas son of Gordias, King of Phrygia" (1.14); note· that Herodotus is careful to fix Gyges in time through written confirmation, having just identified him as a contemporary of the poet Archilochus, who mentioned Gyges in his verses (1.12: first half of the seventh century BC). Herodotus' discussion of Polycrates, the tyrant of Samos in the 540s and 530s BC, makes the distinction even more explicit (3.122): "Polycrates is the first Greek of whom we know to aim at control of the sea, apart from Minos of Knossos and any other before him who may have ruled the sea. But of regular human beings, Polycrates was the first." The phrase "of regular human beings" literally translates as "of human descent:" that is, Minos belongs to the era when the gods were believed to have appeared on earth and to have sired children from mortal women (Minos being the son of Zeus and Europa), while Polycrates was a character of recent history, in which the gods had played no personal or direct role.

In his proem Herodotus places special stress on causation or explanation, saying he will give "particular attention to the reason they went to war with one another." His claim to the title Father of History will therefore depend significantly on how successfully we judge him to have grappled with this central concern of history.

Herodotus' chief word for reason or cause, *aitiê* (the adjective is *aitios*), commonly means "blame" or "responsibility" for wrongs done, although less frequently it is used for good results; it can also mean "cause" or "reason" in a more general sense. Certainly "blame/responsibility" is the meaning that the word carries in the proem. The question "Who is to blame?" is uppermost both in the kidnapping sequence he attributes to the knowledgeable Persians and in his own identification of Croesus as "the first man *I* know of to wrong the Greeks" (1.5). Those who initiate wrongdoing are the ones held responsible, and the wrongdoing expects or requires a response on the part of the injured party. Wrongdoing and retaliation form a unitary process and can apply to the actions of both individuals and groups. But because of the emphasis on blame and because individuals loom large in Herodotus' thinking, some moderns have found his approach to causation naive and simplistic. Yet societies and states described in the *Histories* were dominated far more by monarchs, tyrants and other powerful personalities than today's world is, or seems to be. This is especially true, of course, of an absolute monarchy such as that of Persia. Moreover, retaliation for injuries inflicted (*tisis*) was deemed to be the essence of justice in Greek thinking and in Greek law. It is also part of the larger Greek view of the world described earlier, in which action and counteraction create a balancing tension between opposing forces. We saw evidence for it in Herodotus' view of the natural world and of geography. Here it reappears in the moral world, and forms the foundation of his view of justice, both human and divine.

The first extended narrative of the *Histories*, which concerns Cyrus' conquest of Lydia (1.6–91), illustrates the complexity and diversity of causal explanation in Herodotus. The narrative begins by describing the seizure of the Lydian throne by Croesus' ancestor, Gyges, five generations back. Gyges murdered King Candaules at the prompting of the queen, seized the throne and took the queen for his wife. Gyges' power was confirmed by an oracle from Delphi, which added, however, that Gyges' act of murder would be avenged (*tisis*: 1.13) in the fifth generation. No one, Herodotus says, paid any attention to this pronouncement until it was fulfilled.

The next significant background episode was the visit of the wise Athenian, Solon, to the court of Croesus (an anachronism, since Solon lived ca. 635–ca. 560 BC, Croesus reigned ca. 560–546). After Solon had inspected the immense wealth piled up in Croesus' treasury, the king asked him who he considered the happiest man he had ever seen (Croesus believed he would be the choice). When Solon named quite ordinary Greeks as his first and second choices, the nettled Croesus asked why he, a wealthy monarch, was not among them. Solon replied that he knows god to be jealous of man's prosperity and that one must look to the end of a man's life to see whether he died happily; moreover, great wealth does not ensure happiness and is, in fact, likely to cause its owner the sort of trouble from which a poor man is exempt. "After a promising start god has utterly ruined many a prosperous man" (1.32). Croesus dismisses Solon as "quite silly" (1.33), but "after Solon's departure great retribution (*nemesis*) from god seized upon Croesus because—to make a conjecture—he thought himself the happiest of men" (1.34). A dream then warns Croesus that his son and heir would be killed by an iron spear. Croesus does everything he can to avoid the dream's fulfillment, but to no avail. In the end he forgives the unwitting killer of his son and fixes the blame (*aitios*) on "some god who warned me before of what was to happen" (1.45).

The sequence of events having to do with Cyrus himself then begins. Croesus sees Cyrus' expanding power and decides he must try to check it before it becomes too great: a defensive motive (1.46). Croesus then decides to seek the advice of several oracles, eventually fixing on the oracle of Apollo at Delphi as the most reliable. "He propitiated the god with a lavish sacrifice . . . expecting thereby to win great favor from him" (1.50). Croesus also sent many costly gifts to Delphi before asking Apollo a double question: should he march against Persia and, if so, should he seek an ally? To the first the oracle replied that in marching against Persia he would destroy a mighty empire, to the second that he should seek an alliance with the most powerful Greek state (1.53). Croesus' expectations were greatly encouraged by these responses, and he was prompted to ask another question: would he enjoy a long reign? The oracle replied that Croesus' only fear should be if a mule should sit upon the throne of Persia. This response pleased Croesus even more than the others; he did not expect a mule ever would be king of the Persians and so concluded that he and his descendants would be in power forever (1.56). After making an alliance with Sparta, Croesus, "not understanding what the oracle meant" (1.71), was preparing to attack Cyrus when an adviser named Sandanis tried to dissuade him: Persia was a poor country from which Croesus would get no benefit, whereas Lydia was a rich prize for the impoverished Persians. Croesus rejects the advice of this "wise adviser" figure (which, Herodotus assures us, was quite true: before the conquest of Lydia, Persia was a poor country).

Then Herodotus adds three more motives: Croesus wanted to extend his territory (as opposed to, or in addition to, the defensive reason cited earlier), he trusted the oracle and he wanted to take vengeance (*tisis*) for the deposition by Cyrus of his own brother-in-law Astyages from the throne of Media (1.73). So Croesus invaded Cyrus' territory and met him in a battle from which neither emerged as the winner. Croesus blamed the smaller size of his army for his failure to defeat Cyrus and, when on the following day Cyrus did not venture to march out against him, Croesus decided to return to his capital Sardis and to call on the aid of several allies, including Sparta. They were to assemble at Sardis in four months, at which time he would march against Cyrus in much greater force. He disbanded his army and sent his mercenary soldiers home (1.77).

Cyrus, learning of Croesus' intention to disband his army, decided to advance quickly upon Sardis. He took Croesus by surprise, who nevertheless fielded a Lydian army whose chief strength was its cavalry. But Cyrus employed the ruse of sending camels in among the horses, who took fright and ran off upon seeing and smelling the camels (no horse, Herodotus assures us, can stand a camel). Sardis itself was then put under siege, and was taken by scaling a cliff so precipitous that it was left unguarded. The way up was discovered by a member of Cyrus' army who happened to notice a Lydian soldier scrambling to fetch his helmet that had tumbled down the slope. "So the Persians captured Sardis and took Croesus prisoner, who had ruled for fourteen years and had been besieged for fourteen days, and, just as the oracle had said, had destroyed a mighty empire—his own" (1.86).

Cyrus then placed Croesus on a funeral pyre; the deposed monarch groaned as he realized the truth of Solon's admonition never to count a man happy until he was dead. Cyrus heard his lament and ordered that the fire be extinguished and Croesus brought down from the pyre, "having changed his mind and acknowledging that he, a human being, was about to burn alive another human being who had once been no less fortunate than he, and also fearful of retaliation (*tisis*) and reckoning that there was nothing sure in human affairs" (1.86). But the fire had taken hold too much to be put out; so Croesus called upon Apollo to save him, and from a clear sky a cloudburst extinguished the flames. In the conversation between Cyrus and Croesus that followed, Croesus laid the blame (*aitios*, 1.87) on Apollo, who by his prophecies had encouraged him to attack Cyrus. The Persian king permitted Croesus to send to Delphi to ask if the god were not ashamed to have issued such oracles. The reply came back: even Apollo could not escape destiny (*moira*); Croesus in the fifth generation was fated to pay for the crime of his ancestor Gyges; Apollo had tried to persuade the Fates (*Moirai*) not to have the fall of Sardis occur during Croesus' reign and had succeeded in extending his fall for three years—but, alas, it was not enough (1.91). As for the oracles, Croesus foolishly failed to ask which "mighty empire" was meant; he therefore had only himself to blame (*aitios*). Finally, the oracle about the mule referred to Cyrus, whose parents were from two different nations, his mother a noble Mede, daughter of Astyages, his father a Persian then subject to the Medes. "This was the reply the oracle made to the Lydians, who returned to Sardis and told Croesus. And he, on hearing it, recognized the mistake was his, not that of the god" (1.91).

So ends Herodotus' account of Croesus' downfall. Two features are at once noteworthy. First, the chain of explanation is complex, for it seems to operate on both the human and divine level. Second, Herodotus nowhere distinguishes between more and less important causes as such. Croesus begins by thinking he will check the growing power of Persia before it becomes too dangerous, but after being encouraged by the oracles, he switches to offensive hopes: he wants to add to his territories. In addition, he wishes to avenge the downfall of

45

his brother-in-law Astyages at the hands of Cyrus. All these we might label "long-range" causes (although Herodotus does not describe them as such: they explain why Croesus decided to attack Cyrus in the first place). The more immediate causes are clearly delineated by Herodotus, all of which are military in nature; they explain why Croesus ended by losing his kingdom. Croesus makes two major errors: first, invading Cyrus' territory with a smaller army than the one Cyrus fielded and without the support of the allies he had previously won to his side; second, returning to Sardis and disbanding his army. Cyrus, in turn, made two successful moves: first, his swift pursuit of Croesus to Sardis after learning of the demobilization of Croesus' army; second, sending at the suggestion of one of his captains camels in among the cavalry, the contingent he feared most in the Lydian army. Finally, the fortuitous incident of the retrieved helmet explains why the siege of Sardis lasted but fourteen days.

These causes combine to form a rather full explanation of Croesus' decision to attack Cyrus and of the subsequent loss of his own kingdom. Especially prominent is the psychological factor: Croesus' increasing confidence is carefully delineated, and is specifically and repeatedly emphasized as a cause by Herodotus. Overconfidence leads Croesus to reject the advice of Sandanis against invading Persia and to underestimate his opponent. His reaction to the oracle about the mule is particularly revealing, for from it Croesus got the notion that "neither he nor his descendants would ever cease to rule" (1.56). To a Greek such thinking would have been like an alarm bell going off. Both the world of men and the phenomenal world were ever prone to change: nothing remains the same, and a man must look to the end—particularly, as Solon said, the prosperous man.

But what of the divine element in the story, particularly the oracles? Oracles were, of course, a fact of both the Greek and non-Greek world: men consulted them and acted upon them. Dreams also, which were often thought to be sent by the gods, were similarly believed in and acted upon. Herodotus emphatically states his belief in the truth of oracles when they are clearly expressed: he will not himself say anything against them and will not listen to those who do (8.77). Of course, he realizes that some are highly ambiguous, others deliberately meant to deceive the foolish (e.g. 1.158–159) and still others forged (e.g. 7.6); even Delphi could be bribed (5.63, 90; 6.123). Yet it is doubtful that even "true" oracles are evidence for the hand of god at work in history. Events seldom occur *because* an oracle says they will: that is, because the oracle itself (or the deity behind it) is the causative agent. Most oracles in Herodotus are the momentary raising of the curtain behind which the future waits and the statement of what was glimpsed; they are causative in the sense that when men hear them they often act upon them, as Croesus did when he learned of Apollo's oracle about destroying a mighty empire. But these are human responses to human questions; a god's hidden hand is not at work.

On the other hand, the oracle confirming the power of Gyges and his descendants on the throne of Lydia down to the fifth generation was not a motive for behavior: no one remembered it and no one acted upon it. Yet it came true, as Delphi informed Croesus. In this case a kind of cause and effect seems operative. Gyges committed a murder, which in Greek thinking called for retaliation. And this is exactly how Delphi represents it: retribution (*tisis*: 1.13) would come, but in the fifth generation. The oracle's final response again makes the connection clear, even though here Apollo shifts the responsibility from himself to the Fates (1.91). The thinking that lies behind this explanation is that an offense against the moral order, such as murder, calls for retaliation; such retaliation was sometimes attributed, at least in part, to a specific god, deity in general or fate/destiny. But a response is to be expected, however delayed it may be and whatever the agent(s). Yet even if we believe the "hand of god" to be somehow at work in this case, it is not arbitrary or confined to the supernatural. A human act is the triggering mechanism. Moreover, retaliation is worked out on the human level and is explicable in human terms. Croesus' downfall is the culmination of two quite separate sequences: his own ambition and folly on the one hand, and the retribution for Gyges' murder of Candaules on the other. Nowhere in this story is the divine seen to be manipulating a person against his own will. Quite the contrary: human volition and desire are what initiate the action.

A second causal sequence—that concerning Xerxes' decision to invade Greece (7.1–18)—offers some of the same or analogous motives that we saw in Croesus' case, but also some that are different. One of them is quite puzzling. The narrative in these opening chapters of Book 7 comprises the most detailed and carefully elaborated sequence in the *Histories*: lengthy speeches in a series of council scenes as well as in the bedroom of the Persian monarch. Herodotus depicts Xerxes as initially a more passive figure than Croesus: hot-tempered and young (in fact, he was probably in his late thirties), vacillating and suggestible.

Xerxes at the start of his reign is concerned with suppressing a rebellion in Egypt, not with an invasion of Greece (7.5). His cousin

Mardonius is the one who urges the expedition. He cites several motives: Xerxes will make Athens pay the penalty for her aggression, he will win fame and he will deter others from attacking Persia. In addition, the conquest of a rich and fertile country will be a worthy prize for the monarch of Persia (Greece was, in fact, poor in money and resources). Herodotus adds that Mardonius aimed at being appointed satrap, or governor, of the new territory. Other figures then emerge to support the same course of action. Letters from the reigning family of Thessaly promise its support; members of the Athenian Pisistratid family, in exile at Xerxes' court, seek their return through Xerxes' help; an oracle collector, also at the court, who earlier in his career at Athens was caught in the act of forging oracles, is at present concocting predictions promising success should Xerxes undertake the invasion. Under these pressures, and after he had put down the rebellion in Egypt, "Xerxes was persuaded to march against Greece" (7.7).

After he had been won over, Xerxes summoned the Persian nobles to a meeting in order to discover their opinions and to declare his intentions. In his opening address he sets forth his motives: from his predecessors on the throne he had inherited the legacy of adding to Persian power, and he is determined to equal their achievements; he would add to the glory of them all; he would conquer a land even richer than Persia; he would avenge (*tisis*) the outrage done by Athens to his countrymen and to his father Darius. Mardonius in a flattering reply strongly endorses Xerxes' intent; he emphasizes the ease with which Persia will overwhelm Greece, choosing now to depict Greece as impoverished and undermanned (7.9).

No one ventures to present a contrary argument until Xerxes' uncle Artabanus rises to speak. He cites the Scythian expedition of his brother Darius, which he had urged the king not to undertake: Darius lost many men, failed to conquer Scythia and nearly lost his life in his retreat back across the Danube. Xerxes, too, should abandon his plan to mount an invasion that will take him so far from home, bridging the Hellespont en route; as for Mardonius, he should cease to speak falsehoods about the fighting prowess of the Greeks. Turning back to Xerxes, he continues:

> You see how god strikes with his thunderbolts creatures that stand above the rest and removes them from his sight, but the small ones do not provoke him. You see how he is forever hurling his bolts upon the highest buildings and the tallest trees. For god loves to cut down all things that stand above the rest. So also

48

in the case of a great army: it is destroyed by a small one whenever god in his jealousy makes it fearful or thunderstruck, whereby it perishes unworthily. For god suffers pride in none but himself.

(7.10)

When Artabanus is finished Xerxes turns on him, accusing him of cowardice. What is more, he asserts that if he does not attack Athens first, Athens will invade Persia: the issue is either/or, and there is no middle course. At the end he again cites the motive of retaliation for wrongs suffered (7.11). But after the council session and before going to bed that evening Xerxes turns over in his mind what Artabanus had said. He comes to the conclusion that it would be unwise to mount the invasion.

The tale then takes an unexpected turn. Herodotus declares that, according to the Persians, when Xerxes fell asleep a tall and handsome figure appeared to him in a dream, telling him not to change his mind but to persist in his original design to march against Greece. When Xerxes awoke he paid no attention to the dream but called the Persians together again and told his delighted audience that he was abandoning his plans.

The next night the same figure appeared to him as he slept; it rebuked him for ignoring its behest, ending with this threat (7.14): "Know this well: if you do not immediately mount this invasion, this is what will happen to you: just as you have grown great and powerful in a short time, so shall you quickly be brought low again." Xerxes bounded from his bed in fear and immediately summoned Artabanus:

> If the one who sent this message is a god and it is his pleasure that there be an expedition to Greece, this same dream will also come to you and give the same command as it did to me. I will know that this is so if you don your full regalia, sit on my throne and then sleep in my bed.
>
> (7.15)

Artabanus is reluctant. Xerxes, he says, followed the better course in taking his advice: he himself was not so much bothered in the council meeting by the king's belittling him as by his choosing a course "more likely to lead yourself and the Persians to disaster," one that "increases a man's insolence" and "teaches the soul always to seek more than it has" (7.16). What is more, dreams do not come from the gods, Artabanus explains, but are simply reflections of one's daytime

49

thoughts: in this case, the expedition. But he concedes that, should the dream come to himself if he takes the king's place, or frequently thereafter to Xerxes, then it is likely to have been divinely sent.

So Artabanus ends by agreeing to impersonate the king; and as he sleeps, the same figure appears to him as well:

> Are you the one who dissuaded Xerxes from marching against Greece, as if you were concerned for his welfare? You shall not escape punishment either now or in the future for trying to avert what must happen; Xerxes himself has been shown that he will suffer should he not harken to what must be done.
>
> (7.17)

As the phantom prepares to burn out Artabanus' eyes with hot pokers, Artabanus leaps from the bed and seeks out the king:

> My lord, in my lifetime I have seen many great empires fall to weaker ones. I consequently tried in every way to prevent youthful passion from gaining ascendancy over you, for great covetousness is bad for a man; I remembered how Cyrus' expedition against the Massagetae fared, as well as that of Cambyses against the Ethiopians, while I myself took part in the one Darius mounted against the Scythians. The realization of these things made me believe that by keeping the peace you would be most fortunate among men. That is what I thought. But some divine force is at work here, some disaster sent by the gods is fastening, it seems, upon the Greeks. So I have done a turnabout and have changed my mind. Tell the Persians of the visions sent from god. Bid them follow your original orders for the expedition. So act that nothing on your part is left wanting, since god has given his blessing.
>
> (7.18)

How are we to interpret this puzzling sequence? At the conclusion of the council scene Xerxes is determined on the expedition, and Herodotus has clearly and fully set forth what has caused him to take this decision. The dream episode does not advance the "plot," for at its end we are back at the point where we were before: Xerxes will march on Greece. Yet it is so fully and emphatically developed that it cannot be dismissed as inconsequential (the literary model is the false dream Zeus sends to Agamemnon in the *Iliad* 2.1–47). Some divine power forces Xerxes to change from a safe course that on sober reflection he preferred to a plan that will prove his undoing. In other words, he is being forced to act against his will and to his detriment. The "hand of god" is incontestably at work, seemingly arbitrary, even inscrutable.

The only other major example in the *Histories* of a man endeavoring to escape a bad end but unable to succeed is Polycrates, tyrant of Samos (3.39–43). His ally Amasis, king of Egypt, becomes worried by Polycrates' extraordinary prosperity because he knows, as he writes in a letter, that god is jealous of such a condition. To avoid this jealousy, he wishes for himself and those dear to him a life in which success alternates with failure (3.40): "I have never yet heard of a wholly prosperous man who did not come to an utterly bad end." He advises Polycrates to rid himself of whatever he values most, which Polycrates does: he casts his emerald signet ring into the sea. But a few days later a fisherman presents Polycrates with a huge fish, inside which the ring is found. Polycrates, believing the hand of god to be at work, writes to Amasis of what has happened. The Egyptian, realizing that one man cannot save another from impending disaster and that Polycrates would come to a bad end given his unbroken prosperity, breaks off the friendship: he does this, he says, to avoid the distress he would feel for Polycrates if they were still friends when disaster overtakes him (3.43). And Amasis' fears were well founded: Polycrates later suffers a horrible death (3.120–125).

There are some significant parallels among the episodes of Croesus, Xerxes and Polycrates. The jealousy of god is a factor in all three (1.32, 7.10, 3.40): it is provoked when individuals, natural objects or nations become overly large and flourishing. The divine suffers nothing to rival it in size and good fortune, whereas insignificant things in nature and history, as Artabanus says, do not provoke this jealousy. When excess occurs, imbalance results: equilibrium is restored by cutting the offending object down to size or by eliminating it altogether.

What lies behind this thinking, I suggest, is a variation on the idea of *kosmos* that we have seen before: just as in the natural world and in geography, so in the moral sphere and history, a balance is maintained among opposing forces. Not infrequently Herodotus specifies the divine as the agent responsible for ensuring this stability. When discussing the balance of nature at 3.108, for example, he attributes it to "the forethought of god, being wise, as it certainly seems to be." Most often excess is seen in terms of sheer size, whether in bulk, wealth or territory. Rarely Herodotus seems willing to believe that one's mental attitude alone or primarily is sufficient to provoke divine displeasure; an example is at 1.34, where Croesus loses his son and heir "because—to make a conjecture—he thought himself the happiest of men."

In his account of Xerxes' dream, as in the case of Polycrates, Herodotus emphasizes that great good fortune and prosperity are sufficient to bring an offender low. The offender's *intention* is immaterial: both tyrant and monarch have simply grown too great, and if they are unable or do not care to pare down their size and power by their own efforts, another force—the divine—will see to it. In Xerxes' case it would seem that mere quiescence is not enough to ensure his welfare; Persia is already oversized, and it is the nation more than the monarch that is the crux of the difficulty. This may be the reason that the dream forces him to go even after he has decided against it; and from the length and emphasis Herodotus gives the episode this may be the point that he wants to make. Moreover, if the divine can be roused to action by simple arrogance, as Herodotus was inclined to think applied to Croesus, Xerxes' attitude as expressed in the council scene would send chills of apprehension down any Greek's spine, for it is an open invitation to disaster:

> If we vanquish these people [the Athenians] and their neighbors in the Peloponnesus, we will make Persia's borders coextensive with god's own sky. For the sun will look down upon no nation that borders ours, but as I pass through the whole of Europe I shall make a single country of them, along with you. I have come to realize that, once the people I have mentioned are out of the way, no human city, no nation of men will be left that will be able to oppose us. Thus I shall put under the yoke of slavery both those who are to blame (*aitios*) and those who are not.
>
> (7.8)

Herodotus' narrative of events immediately following this conversation between Xerxes and Artabanus details a series of acts on the part of the Persian king as he marches to the Hellespont that illustrate his pride and willfulness. The first was to make the peninsula of Mt Athos into an island by digging a canal at its isthmus. He could easily have dragged his boats over the narrow neck of land, Herodotus observes (7.24), but it is the historian's guess that his motive was simply to show off his power and leave a memorial of himself. Such an extravagant attempt to alter nature would have struck many Greeks as likely to provoke divine displeasure. When the people of Cnidos, for example, attempted to cut through the narrow isthmus connecting them to the Asiatic mainland (in order to avert Persian subjugation), the diggers experienced a great number of mishaps. Delphi was consulted. Apollo ordered them to cease the digging, saying, "Zeus would have made it an island, if this were his wish" (1.174). Xerxes' execution of Pythius' youngest son comes after the cutting of the Athos canal, followed in turn by the episode of decorating a handsome plane tree with golden ornaments (7.27–31). Xerxes then comes to the Hellespont, where the first bridge between Asia and Europe that he had ordered constructed had been swept away in a storm. In his anger the king ordered that the Hellespont receive three hundred lashes and that those plying the whips curse the waters (an act that Herodotus describes as "barbarian and presumptuous," 7.35). In addition, a pair of fetters was thrown in it and the waters branded. Finally, the builders of the first bridge were beheaded.

From all of this Xerxes' megalomania is made manifest. At the Hellespont itself, as he prepares to march his army over the rebuilt bridge, Xerxes has another conversation with Artabanus. At first the king bursts into tears as he realizes that in a hundred years all the thousands he sees before him will be dead. He then asks his uncle whether he would have persisted in his opposition to the expedition if the figure in the dream had not appeared to him. Artabanus prays that all will turn out well, but confesses his foreboding. Xerxes cannot understand: is his army not large enough? Artabanus replies that its great size is precisely what he fears: by sea no harbor will be large enough to accommodate the fleet, by land the increasing distance from home will put the huge army in danger of starvation: "Know that circumstances control men, not men circumstances," he cautions (7.49). In response Xerxes admits that Artabanus' remarks are sensible, but asserts that he is too timid: if Xerxes' predecessors on the throne had not been aggressive and had not taken risks, there would be no Persian Empire today. The king bids his uncle to take heart and to adopt an optimistic attitude: he will conquer the whole of Europe (7.50), a vow he repeats in his prayer to the sun as he prepares to cross from Asia to Europe (7.54).

The theme is clear: large empires, like tall trees, high buildings and great prosperity, will be cut down to size. And sheer numbers literally prove Xerxes' undoing. Even at the Battle of Thermopylae, his huge force could not of itself prevail in the narrow pass; a detachment led by the traitor Ephialtes to the defenders' rear was what enabled Xerxes to win. At the Battle of Salamis the many large vessels of the Persian fleet rammed one another in the confined bay, proving more a cause of the defeat than the efforts of the smaller Greek boats (8.83–90). In the earlier battle off the promontory at Artemisium, which was the naval counterpart to the fight at Thermopylae by land, Herodotus is at pains to emphasize the disparity between the two forces: the Greek ships were fewer and slower, the Persian much more numerous and faster (8.10). The Greeks prevailed nevertheless; but that night a violent storm caused much greater destruction. Herodotus interprets the significance of the storm in this way (8.13): "God was doing everything to make the Persian fleet more the size of the Greek and reduce its superiority." On the next day the Persian commanders engaged the Greeks again because they were ashamed of having been worsted by a smaller fleet and because they feared Xerxes' punishment. But the very size of the ships and their greater numbers proved their undoing as they rammed one another in close formation (8.16)—a foreshadowing of the coming battle at Salamis.

The foregoing examination of causation has devoted considerable space to the divine element in Herodotus because we in this age find the subject difficult to understand. But the length of the discussion overprivileges the importance of the topic in the *Histories* as a whole: the "hand of god" in fact appears infrequently, although admittedly at some crucial points in the narrative. The large majority of events occur because of the calculations, passions and actions of men alone. The gods are often invoked when normative explanations on the human level are inadequate, as in the case of Helen, mentioned earlier (2.120).

Perhaps the clearest example concerns what Herodotus calls "the wrath of Talthybius" (7.133–137: Talthybius was the herald of King Agamemnon at Troy and had his own temple in Sparta). Heralds or ambassadors in the Greek and non-Greek world were regarded as sancrosanct and inviolable, but when Darius around 492 BC sent envoys to Athens and Sparta to demand their submission, each city put to death the ambassadors sent to it. In the case of Sparta, when their sacrifices did not go well subsequent to the murder of the ambassadors, they decided to send to Xerxes (who had recently succeeded to the throne) two men who were willing to sacrifice their lives in recompense for the crime (*tisis*, 7.134). Xerxes magnanimously spared their lives. During the Peloponnesian War some fifty years later the sons of the two Spartans whose lives Xerxes had spared were acting as ambassadors of their country. They were seized and sent to Athens, where they were killed. This event Herodotus believes to be emphatically divine in origin (*theiotaton*), a manifestation of the wrath of Talthybius: the punishment fell precisely upon ambassadors and precisely upon the sons of those sent to expiate the original crime:

"It is clear to me that god had a hand in the matter," he concludes (7.134). For him the double coincidence was so extraordinary and improbable that he believes it could only be divine in origin.

Contrast this with his comment on what befell Athens. He says he cannot say for certain what terrible thing happened to the Athenians as a consequence of the murder of Darius' ambassadors. City and territory were ravaged under Xerxes, to be sure, but he is inclined to think the murder of Darius' ambassadors was *not* the cause (*aitiê*, 7.133). Here there were no improbable coincidences and hence no compelling reason to assign a divine agent as the cause of punishment. So he refuses to assign one.

Herodotus sees an overarching pattern in history. He introduces the theme at the very start of his work. After reviewing the account of the kidnapped women according to the "knowledgeable Persians" to explain the enmity between East and West, he says:

> I am not going to say whether these events happened in this or some other way, but after naming the man *I* know to have first wronged the Greeks, I shall go forward with my story, mentioning in my journey cities of men, great and small alike; for most of those that formerly were great have now become small, and those that have grown great in my time once were small. So, knowing that human prosperity never remains the same, I shall mention both alike.
>
> (1.5)

These patterns are not cyclical in the sense of being consistent or uniform, for the rise of great individuals and states, together with egregious wrongdoing such as sacrilege and murder, cannot be predicted: their occurrence is irregular. But once excessive growth or misdeeds occur, one can confidently anticipate that sooner or later the offenders will be brought low.

Two closely linked paradigms that explain the rise and fall of states and individuals underlie this conception of historical change in the *Histories*. The first can be seen in some of Greek tragedy, and constitutes a "tragic pattern" of sorts. Continuous good fortune leads to fullness or satiety (*koros*: the metaphor is one of eating). The excessive prosperity that results engenders insolence or arrogance (*hybris*) that manifests itself in attitude, speech and/or action. Often cautionary advice or a prediction of disaster is given (e.g. by a Teiresias, Cassandra or dream), but the warning figure is ignored or disbelieved. Once the person has overstepped the proper limits allotted to himself as a mortal (*moira*), his doom is sealed (*atê*). Punishment ensues, sometimes personified as Justice (*Dikê*) or Retribution (*Nemesis* or *Adrasteia*). The influence of tragedy on Herodotus is felt not only in such themes, but through many other dramatic conventions. A clear instance concerns the death of Croesus' son and heir (1.34–45). It is narrated in a series of discrete scenes, enlivened with speech and dialogue. There is a warning dream and even a messenger speech (the latter being one of the staples of tragedy, coming at the point when disaster is announced). Even some of the names in this tale have a tragic flavor: the son is Atys ("Doom"), his killer Adrastus ("Retribution"). Herodotus begin the story as follows(1.34): "After Solon's departure, great retribution [*nemesis megalê*] from god seized upon Croesus, because—to make a conjecture—he thought himself the happiest of men."

This tragic pattern is not confined to self-contained episodes, but extends over long stretches of the *Histories*. It can easily be traced, for example, in the lengthy narratives concerning Croesus' fall and Xerxes' defeat. The career of Cyrus in Book 1 is another illustration. After his success against Croesus he conquers the wealthy and civilized city of Babylon, at which point two motives spur him to go further (1.204): first, the story of his birth, which seemed to be greater than that of an ordinary mortal (recounted at 1.108–113); second, his great good fortune against all those against whom he had fought. So Cyrus decides to march against the backward and warlike tribe of the Massagetae, a nation of nomads ruled by Queen Tomyris. Two warning figures appear. The first is Croesus, now a part of Cyrus' entourage. He has learned, he says, from his own misfortunes. Furthermore,

> If you think you are immortal and the army you lead is also, there would be little point in my telling you my opinion. But if you realize that you are a human being and are a single man at the head of an army of human beings, know first that there is a cycle [*kuklos*] in human affairs and as it moves round it does not allow the same people always to be fortunate.
>
> (1.207)

The second warning figure is Queen Tomyris herself. After part of her army is defeated and her son captured, she tells Cyrus in a letter to leave her realm while he has a chance to escape (1.212). She is made to adopt the language of Greek tragedy by describing him as "insatiable for blood" and committing an act of insolence (*hybris*) in the way he has defeated her forces; she ends by saying that if he does not clear out, "I will sate (*koros*) your insatiable bloodlust." Cyrus is defeated; the Queen has a search made for his body and plunges his severed head into an animal skin filled with human blood. "I told you I would sate you with blood, and I have!" she cries as Book 1 reaches its climax (1.214).

The second paradigm, closely associated with the first, is the contrast between "hard" and "soft" cultures to explain the rise and fall of states in the *Histories*. These are modern terms, but fit well with Herodotus' general views and, sometimes, even his language. Hard cultures tend to be backward, poor, unwelcoming, lacking in a strong central government and vigorously independent. Scythia is the prime example; another is the Massagetae (who some thought were a branch of the Scythians: 1.201). Soft cultures are civilized, wealthy and seductive, often ruled by absolute monarchs and vulnerable to conquest from without (frequently employing mercenaries). Egypt is the chief illustration (so also Lydia and Babylon).

Relatively stable hard and soft cultures tend to occur toward the edges of the known world (Egypt and Scythia are alike in that neither borrows customs from its neighbors: 2.79, 91; 4.76). The center is open to influence from outside, and presents a mixture in climate and culture (e.g. Persia and Greece). Yet hard and soft cultures are not monolithic or static, especially those near the center, but are subject to the dynamics of historical change. Such dynamics lead certain hard cultures to expand at the expense of soft cultures, taking them over and assimilating them (there are no examples in the *Histories* of soft cultures conquering hard ones). But in the process of assimilation they themselves become soft: the wealth and luxury of the defeated gradually sap the original vigor of the conqueror. Persia is the prime example. At the start she is poor and backward, as Sandanis tells Croesus when trying to dissuade him from attacking Cyrus (1.71). Conquests of countries such as Lydia, Babylon and Egypt greatly enrich Persia and have a profound influence on her in other ways as well: "Of all men," Herodotus says, "the Persians are the most accepting of foreign customs [*nomoi*]" (1.135). She begins to lose her effectiveness when confronting hard peoples, such as the Massagetae. Then comes Darius' unsuccessful attempt to conquer Scythia, the exemplar par excellence of a hard culture in the *Histories*. Finally comes Greece herself, which is depicted as a relatively hard country in comparison to what Persia has developed into. Demaratus tells Xerxes

(7.102): "Poverty has always been part of Greece's inheritance, whereas her valor has been acquired; valor has been fashioned out of wisdom and powerful *nomos* and because of it Greece keeps both poverty and despotism at bay." After his defeat at Salamis Xerxes flees back to his homeland where, as Herodotus describes in the last book, frightful court intrigues plague and cripple the monarchy still further (9.108–113). Also near the end is a telling anecdote concerning the Spartan king Pausanias, victor over Mardonius at the Battle of Plataea (9.82). When Pausanias saw the splendid riches he had captured from the Persians, he ordered the cooks to prepare the kind of dinner they would have served to Mardonius, while, as a joke, he instructed his own cooks to prepare a typical Spartan meal. He summoned the other Greek commanders to see the results, saying, "Men of Greece, the reason I invited you here is to demonstrate the folly of the Persians: possessed of the delicacies you see over there, they came to deprive us of this miserable stuff!"

Then comes the final episode of the *Histories*, the siege and fall of Sestos on the Hellespont. Its Persian commander, Artayctes, is captured and put to death, which leads to Herodotus' concluding anecdote—one that resonates ironically back through the work, to its very inception:

> Artayctes . . . had an ancestor Artembares who made the following proposal to the Persians, who in turn put it before Cyrus: "Since Zeus has given hegemony to the Persians and to you in particular, Cyrus, by your defeat of Astyages, come, let us leave the small and rough land we now possess and occupy another and better one. There are many such nearby and many further off; if we occupy one of them we will be more impressive in all sorts of ways. It is natural for men in power to do such a thing—and when will there be a better opportunity than now, when we rule many men and all of Asia?" Cyrus on hearing this was not impressed by the proposal. He bid them to act on it, but on the understanding that they should be prepared no longer to rule but to be ruled: for from soft countries come soft men, since the same land does not produce impressive crops and good warriors. The result was that the Persians were convinced and departed, deferring to Cyrus' opinion. They chose to live in a poor land and rule than to sow the plain and be slaves to others.
>
> (9.122)

A final word on the scope of Herodotus' achievement. A number of historians in Greece and Rome wrote much more and covered many more years than he did. But scarcely any came close to matching the breadth of his world view. Most of these later historians, however voluminous, were content to narrate the history of their own peoples, whether Greeks or Romans, and to do so with jingoistic parochialism. They had little knowledge of or interest in foreign peoples for their own sake. Herodotus is the shining exception. He saw how the great empires of the East, such as Egypt, Assyria, Babylon and Persia, fitted into a grand historical scheme; moreover, he was curious and keenly interested in their lands, customs and history. Naturally he observed them from a Greek viewpoint and was writing for a Greek audience. And if he did not succeed very often in penetrating into their several *mentalitées*, he at least was aware that they existed and made an effort at times to describe cultural biases in his *Histories*: the conversations between Xerxes and Demaratus comprise the most striking illustration. Plutarch in his essay "On the Malice of Herodotus" called the historian *philobarbaros*: "a barbarian lover." Plutarch meant it as a reproach. For us today it seems a high compliment.

4

THUCYDIDES
Subject and methods

Thucydides was born some twenty-five years after Herodotus, in the early 450s BC. Yet the works of the two men are so different from one another, to say nothing of background and temperament, that many generations seem to separate them, not one. No doubt the chief reason for the difference are those twenty-five years, for in that short time profound changes swept over the Greek world. The Halicarnassus where Herodotus was born ca. 484 BC was a small city on the eastern shore of the Aegean Sea subject to Persia and ruled by a single family that served at Persia's pleasure. The Athens into which Thucydides was born nearly a generation later had become the head of a great maritime empire: what had begun as a voluntary league of equals formed immediately after Xerxes' defeat to drive Persia from her Greek holdings in Ionia had been gradually transformed into an Athenian empire whose members paid tribute to the dominant city and, if they attempted to quit the alliance, were forced to rejoin it. Halicarnassus became a small part of that empire, which dominated almost the whole of the Aegean Sea and its littoral: some two hundred states were members.

Athens herself was a radical democracy run by an assembly composed of all adult male citizens and a council of five hundred (the Boulê) that prepared the agenda of the assembly and ran the day-to-day business of the state, together with the ten chief magistrates, called archons. The archons, the members of the Boulê and all jurors were selected annually by lot from among the adult male citizens. The only officials actually elected were the ten generals, or *stratêgoi*, who were in charge of military operations on land and sea. The city was a large and thriving metropolis whose overall population included many slaves and resident foreigners, styled metics. But only the adult males discussed, voted and served the state. It has been estimated that some 300,000 people were resident in Athens at the start of the Peloponnesian War in 431 BC and that the adult male citizens comprised roughly fifteen percent of the whole.

Thucydides was born into a prominent aristocratic Athenian family. His father's name of Olorus (4.104), which is non-Greek, links him to the great Athenian military leader Miltiades and his family, the Philaidae. Miltiades had married the daughter of the wealthy Thracian king Olorus around 512 BC; from this union came Cimon, a commanding figure in Athenian politics and in the creation of the Athenian empire, who died in 449. The Greek practice of carrying down names in the family makes it almost certain that the historian was related by blood to Cimon, and hence belonged to a group sometimes opposed in Athenian politics to Pericles and the family of the Alcmaeonidae. Thucydides' admiration for Pericles, therefore (2.65), is noteworthy and testifies to his independence of judgment.

Thucydides caught the plague that swept through Athens in the first years of the war, but recovered (2.48). Elected general for the year 424, he was posted in the area of Thrace in the north Aegean, where because of family connections he possessed the right of working the gold mines and had much influence among the inhabitants (4.104). The Spartan general Brasidas made a surprise assault upon the chief city of the area, the Athenian colony of Amphipolis. He seized the place from Thucydides' colleague, the *stratêgos* Eucles; the historian, who was in charge of a naval contingent on the nearby island of Thasos, sailed at once. He managed to secure Amphipolis' port city of Eion before it fell into Brasidas' hands. But he did not save Amphipolis, and for this failure Thucydides went into exile, which lasted for the twenty years that remained in the war (5.26). He returned to Athens at its end (404 BC), but appears not to have survived long, dying sometime shortly after 400 BC.

His history of the Peloponnesian War, which lasted from 431 to 404, is unfinished, breaking off abruptly in the eighth book in the year 411 (the book divisions, while ancient, are not Thucydides' doing). Thucydides must have died suddenly, and we owe publication of the work to a literary executor; a late source identifies him as the historian Xenophon, who continued the narrative of the war in his own work, the *Hellenica*, but the claim is doubtful. In his opening sentence he says he began writing the moment the war broke out, "expecting it would be great and the most worthy of record of those that had gone before." Later he amplifies a bit (5.26): he lived through the twenty-seven-year

61

war, being mature enough to observe it critically and with the intention of securing accurate information; furthermore, he had the opportunity to associate with both parties, but especially the Peloponnesians, because of his exile.

Thucydides' first book is introductory in nature and covers three topics: first, a review of earlier wars in Greek history to show that the present one eclipsed them all in length, scope and calamity; second, a quick and selective review of events of the nearly fifty years that elapsed between the point where Herodotus' history had left off and the Peloponnesian War began; finally, a detailed account of the immediate causes that precipitated the conflict. The first ten years of the war, sometimes called the Archidamian War after the Spartan king and general Archidamus, ended in a draw (Books 2–5.24); the Peace of Nicias of 421 BC marked its end, which Thucydides quotes at 5.18–19. But the peace was unsteady from the start: neither side fulfilled all the provisions to which it had agreed, some allies on both sides did not subscribe to the treaty and, in two local wars centering on the Peloponnesian cities of Mantinea and Epidaurus, violations of the treaty were committed by both Athens and Sparta. When they resumed direct hostilities against one another nearly seven years later, the last phase of the war began. It was ushered in by Athens' invasion of the island of Sicily (415–413 BC: Books 6 and 7), and began in earnest when Sparta seized and permanently occupied the fort at Decelea in Athenian territory (413 BC: often called the Decelean War). Thucydides marks the phases of the war in his so-called second introduction at 5.26. His language strongly suggests that some people did not regard the whole of the twenty-seven years as a single war, but broke it down into several. The historian firmly rejects this view: the treaty of 421 BC ushered in no true peace, he asserts, and the whole of the twenty-seven-year period constituted a unitary sequence.

There has been much discussion whether the history was written in the order in which we now see it, when in his lifetime Thucydides composed it, or parts of it, and, in view of the fact that he did not complete it, whether what survives is fully finished. This has been dubbed the Thucydidean Question, on which more has been written than on any other topic. Some believe, for example, that Thucydides wrote up most of what we now have in the last few years of his life, others that some extended sections date to the early years of the war. If indeed he composed different sections as much as twenty-five years apart, we might expect the historian to have expanded and even changed his views as the war reached its last phases and concluded. For example, some have interpreted the "second introduction," 1, tioned above, as not so much a rejection of the ideas of others as reflection of Thucydides' own somewhat surprised (and delayed) realization that the entire twenty-seven years comprised a single, ongoing conflict. Finally, there is the question of completeness. Thucydides' account of the nearly four-and-a-half-year period in which the Peace of Nicias was ostensibly in effect (5.25–end) not only contains no speeches but includes verbatim extracts of several documents—an unusual procedure in ancient historiography; only the Melian Dialogue at the end contains direct speech (5.85–113). Moreover, what is left of Book 8 (which is considerable) contains the same features: no speeches and the quotation of a number of documents. These two peculiarities have suggested to some that, had Thucydides lived, he would have added speeches and at least have paraphrased the documents. Others think that he was experimenting with new techniques in these sections and intended them to take the form we now see. Cratippus, one of Thucydides' ancient continuators, took this view in respect to the absence of speeches (*FGrH* 64 F1).

The questions of when Thucydides wrote up the various parts of his history and particularly whether his thinking changed during the course of the war are extremely important, but difficult to answer satisfactorily. Of the many theories propounded as solutions to these questions, the present writer does not find any wholly convincing. Although some sections seem to be more finished than others (e.g. the Sicilian expedition in Books 6–7), this is probably due more to the nature of the material than to anything else. On the other hand, Book 8, aside from the absence of speeches and the quotation of documents, and despite its detailed narrative, has a number of features that suggest it is less finished than the other parts of the history, e.g. occasional contradictions in factual reports and uncharacteristic tentativeness at times (8.56, 64, 87). To this reader the rest of the history looks to be in nearly final form, although it would have doubtless been subject to a final revision had Thucydides lived to complete the whole.

Thucydides assumes from the start that his readers are generally acquainted with the government, society and economy of both Athens and Sparta, and with the sort of league each of them headed. It is true that he mentions aspects of these topics here and there, but for an overall view one must piece the bits of information together from him and other ancient sources.

Athens depended almost wholly on her navy for her wealth and

rtly before Xerxes' invasion, it had been the chief
defeats by sea and in the subsequent effort to free
f Ionia from Persian control. The members of the
luntarily formed to expel Persia from Ionia at first
nd crews to the war effort, the number depending
alth of each participant. Although all members
sible equals, Athens was the dominant power because she
supplied the commanding officers and more ships than did the
others. She was by tradition, moreover, the mother city of the Ionians,
for it was from Athens centuries before that Ionia had been colonized.
Over time most members came to prefer to make cash contributions
to the league treasury, situated on the island of Delos, in lieu of
having themselves to build and man the ships. So Athens did it for
them. By the start of the Peloponnesian War only two large island
states, Lesbos and Samos, were still making their contributions in the
form of ships (1.19).

Most of Ionia had been liberated by 467 BC and the primary
mission of the league seemed to have been fulfilled; but when certain
states tried to quit the league, they found themselves without the
military clout to resist successfully Athens' refusal to countenance
defection from what was now in effect an Athenian empire. Athens
encouraged and supported democracies in the member states over
against oligarchies, in order to bring their political sympathies more
in line with her own. In 454 BC the league treasury was moved to
Athens.

Athens' primary reliance on her navy meant that the poorer
Athenian citizens, who supplied the crews for the ships, were a vital
element in the state. Hence it is not surprising that politicians like
Pericles saw to it that their interests were met in the radical democracy
that characterized Athens in the mid- to late fifth century. Not only
were they members of the general assembly of male citizens, which
was the ultimate authority in all matters, but they were paid a daily
wage for their naval service. Attica (the name of the territory of
Athens) had a thin, rocky soil suitable for olive and grape culture, but
not for the production of some other essential items, particularly
grain. Thus many foodstuffs had to be imported in order to feed the
large population. In addition, other materials, such as timber for
shipbuilding, had to be procured from foreign sources. A complex
network of trade routes consequently grew up, especially to the north
Aegean and Black Sea areas and to the wealthy Greek cities in Sicily
and south Italy.

In addition to her wealth and power, Athens acted as a magnet for people from all over the Greek and non-Greek worlds. The resident aliens, or metics, many of whom were skilled craftsmen, nearly equalled the male citizens in number, while the slaves, all of foreign origin, outnumbered the male citizens and metics combined by more than two to one. The city was therefore open to all kinds of cross-currents and new ideas. Traders and items of commerce were in evidence everywhere; intellectuals known as sophists flocked to the city from near and far, dazzling its inhabitants with their learning and verbal legerdemain; philosophers flourished and clashed; partly from the proceeds of the league treasury the Acropolis was rebuilt in a series of monumental buildings that are impressive even in their present ruined state. Literature enjoyed a remarkable flowering, in particular the tragedies of Aeschylus, Sophocles and Euripides and the comedies of Aristophanes. "Our whole city is the school of Greece," Thucydides has Pericles say in his funeral oration (2.41), "For of cities now existing she alone proves when put to the test to be greater than her reputation and alone gives no cause either to an aggressor for chagrin at being worsted by an inferior opponent or to a subject state to complain of rule by an unworthy overlord."

In almost every respect Sparta was the antithesis of Athens. She was considered the leader of the Dorian branch of the Greeks, and spoke a different dialect than did the Ionians. She was above all a land power, possessing the only professional army in Greece. What enabled her to maintain this army of heavy-armed infantry (called hoplites) was the peculiar system attributed to the legendary lawgiver Lycurgus. In Sparta (which is the name of the chief city of Lacedaemon or Laconia) the number of full citizens, known as Spartiates, was quite small; they were supported by a great many state serfs called helots. The helots farmed the estates owned by the Spartiates and gave the owners a portion of the yearly produce. This produce enabled each Spartiate to contribute his share of food to one of the military messes to which he belonged. Up to the age of seven a Spartiate male lived with his mother. From seven to age twenty he joined a large military school in order to learn discipline and undergo rigorous training. When he reached the age of thirty he became a full citizen. Throughout his career army barracks were his living quarters and, although he might marry at age twenty, he could never live with his wife and children as a family.

The chief aim of this peculiar and restrictive system was to maintain a vigilant and efficient military force that would be superior to Sparta's foreign enemies and, most especially, to her chief domestic enemy, the helots. For they vastly outnumbered the Spartiate land-owners and, should they rise up in rebellion, the basis of the Spartan economy would collapse: the work of the helots enabled the Spartiates to devote themselves wholly to soldiering. A revolt of the helots was thus Sparta's greatest fear. In order to keep them under control, the young Spartiates formed the Krypteia, which literally means "secret police," whose activities were sanctioned by the annual declaration of war upon the helots issued by Sparta's chief magistrates, the ephors. The Spartiates numbered only about four thousand in the fifth century; what the number of helots was is unknown, except that they were more numerous in relation to the free population than in any other Greek state. The small number of available Spartiate soldiers during the Peloponnesian War forced them to include helots as fighters at times. But when Athens seized the island of Sphacteria next to Spartan territory and called the helots to revolt, extreme measures were taken. Thucydides reports (4.80) that in 424 BC Sparta invited the helots to select their best fighters so that they could receive their freedom as recompense. Two thousand were picked, every one of whom the Krypteia did away with in the belief that the bravest were the most enterprising and hence most likely to spark a revolt.

The government of Sparta was simple. There were two royal houses and hence two kings. The kings were largely confined to religious duties in peacetime, but in war one was chosen to be commander for a particular campaign. The chief magistrates were five annually elected ephors, who acted as a check upon the kings, even in wartime. They also called into session the Gerousia, or Council of Elders, consisting of twenty-eight men over sixty and the two kings. The assembly was the Spartiates voting by simple acclamation to proposals put to them; there was no debate.

Sparta was therefore a tightly run military state, dependent almost wholly on agriculture for subsistence. Trade was discouraged (cur-rency took the form of heavy iron spits), foreign visitors were viewed with suspicion and from time to time were summarily order to leave en masse. There was no intellectual or artistic life to speak of. The system was designed to cut off the inhabitants from foreign contacts and ideas and to produce tough, highly trained soldiers according to a severe and simple regimen. Spartiates were renowned throughout Greece as superlative fighters, men of old-fashioned morality, slow to act and conservative in the extreme.

Sparta was the head of a loose league of states, mostly situated in the

Peloponnesus, in which each member had one vote; dues or tribute was not imposed. Being an oligarchy herself, she supported oligarchies among her allied states. She also supplied the commanders for the league's military operations and, naturally, contributed its most effective fighting force. Next to Sparta herself the most important member was Corinth, strategically located at the isthmus connecting the Peloponnesus with the rest of mainland Greece, between the Saronic and Corinthian Gulfs. Corinth was wealthy and powerful, an emporium for trade between the eastern and western parts of the Mediterranean. Goods and ships in transit were easily moved over the narrow isthmus from one gulf to the other, thus enabling shippers to avoid the circuitous and perilous voyage around the Peloponnesus.

As Athens expanded her empire and her trade routes, it was almost inevitable that she would come into conflict with Corinth's widespread commercial interests. And so she did, for Corinth was directly involved in the two incidents that in Thucydides' view were the immediate or precipitating causes of the war. The first (1.24–55) concerned Corinth's colony on the island of Corcyra (modern Corfu) located in the Ionian Sea near the entrance to the Gulf of Corinth and a vital way station for shipping headed for Italy and the West. Corcyra possessed the third largest fleet in Greece, Athens having the first and Corinth the second. When Corcyra made overtures at becoming an ally of Athens, Corinth objected strenuously, declaring that as the mother city deference and obedience were owed to her. A military clash into which Athens was drawn ended with Corinth's defeat: that is, she was unable to prevent her colony from allying with Athens. The second (1.56–65) involved another colony of Corinth, Potidaea in the north Aegean. Potidaea was a member of Athens' empire, and when she revolted partly because her tribute had been more than doubled a few years before (not, however, mentioned by Thucydides), Corinth unofficially sent help. Athens besieged the town and eventually retook it. It is not surprising, therefore, that Corinth was the chief instigator in urging the Spartans and the other members of the Peloponnesian League to go to war with Athens.

When hostilities began, the main issue of the war was plain. Sparta and her allies were determined to check the untrammeled growth of Athens. The basic point of dispute in the incident at Corcyra was whether Athens could be permitted to extend her alliances without restraint—in this case to a powerful state far removed from the Aegean, and one that Corinth regarded as belonging to her sphere of influence. The issue at Potidaea was whether a tribute-paying member of Athens' empire, especially a colony founded by Corinth (who even supplied the city's annual chief magistrate), could be forced to sever contact with its mother city and to be part of Athens' empire against its will. In order for Sparta to win the war she had to defeat Athens outright. If she did not, even a fight to a standstill would mean victory for Athens, since Sparta would be shown to be unable to limit Athenian expansion or to interfere in her existing empire.

Athens dominated the sea, but was no match for Sparta and her allies on land. She therefore transformed herself, in effect, into an island. Three parallel walls, known as the Long Walls, connected Athens with her port city of Piraeus, four miles distant. Her defense works were such that she could withstand a siege indefinitely, even should Sparta occupy the rest of Attica, since all foodstuffs and essential materials could be brought in by sea. If one of the walls chanced to be breached, the corridor between the other two would remain. And within the Long Walls would be room for the country population of Attica to find refuge. Hence Pericles persuaded them to move themselves and their possessions within the Long Walls (1.143–144): all Athens had to do to win the war, he said, was to lie low and take no unnecessary risks. The burden of winning lay with Sparta; victory would depend on her becoming a sea power, but for this, he said, she did not have the temperament, expertise or money.

The differences between the works of Greece's first two historians are, as has been said, extreme. This is partly because Thucydides deliberately distanced himself from Herodotus, pointedly rejecting the methods of his predecessor and seeking to transcend his achievement. He is in some sense in competition with Herodotus, as he is to a lesser extent with Homer, the other great chronicler of a great war. The opening section of the first book (1–23), conventionally dubbed the Archaeology, was partly written under the stimulus of this rivalry. Thucydides reviews the previous wars of the Greeks and finds that none of them matches his war in scope, duration or frightfulness. The Trojan and Persian Wars are uppermost in his mind. In the case of the former, he argues, we must allow for poetic exaggeration on Homer's part; even so, it lasted but ten years and only a part of the fighting force was used at any one time, the rest being employed in securing food and supplies (1.10–11). As for the Persian Wars, he concedes that they were greater than those preceding, but at the same time notes that they were quickly decided in two battles by land and two by sea (1.23).

Just before making this rather dismissive appraisal he had inter-

rupted his review of past wars to criticize certain unnamed pe[
accepting popular hearsay about the past without subjectir
critical examination (1.20). They even do this, he contin
matters concerning contemporary history, where the facts
verified, and he cites two errors by way of illustration. Both are to be
found in Herodotus. One is that there is a military company in Sparta
called Pitane, "there being no such thing" (see Herodotus 9.53, cf.
3.55), the other that the Spartan kings have two votes each in the
Gerousia, whereas they have but one (see Herodotus 6.57, where this is
implied rather than expressly stated). "So lacking in industry is the
search for the truth on the part of many people, who are disposed to
accept whatever comes to hand." His history, he continues (1.21), will
be based on reliable evidence and will not be subject to the exaggeration of poets (Homer is the obvious target here) nor to "the privileging
of pleasure over truth on the part of storytellers [*logographoi*] whose
accounts are unverifiable and have in the course of time become
enshrined in the realm of fable and makebelieve." Herodotus is
seemingly his chief target here, whom he unflatteringly classes as a
logographos. He concludes his critique in this way (1.22): "Possibly the
absence of the story-telling element in my history may make it less
entertaining. . . . But my work is a possession for all time, not a
showpiece designed to catch the applause of the moment."

Perhaps the greatest difference between the two historians concerns
scope and focus. Herodotus selected a vast theme as his subject: the rise
of the Persian Empire, followed by the Persian Wars themselves. His
manner of narration led him to include many digressions and amusing
stories, as he candidly confesses; all sorts of subjects find room in his
expansive canvas. Thucydides' focus was one of fierce, laser-like
concentration on a single topic, the war. When it begins, he fixes
its precise date (2.2) and recounts the events of each year by summers
and winters. There are few digressions: topics that do not bear directly
on the war are excluded. The greatest criticism made of Thucydides, in
fact, concerns what he fails to tell us. We would never know of the
great intellectual and artistic flowering in fifth-century Athens had
we to rely on him, for example. Even matters that we today view as
significant factors affecting the war either find no place or are given
short shrift in his pages. There is little, for example, on the complex
and delicate logistics that were required to supply Athens with food
and essential war materials from abroad. Nor do we find much about
the status and obligations of her allies. Inscriptional evidence shows,
for instance, that in 425/424 BC Athens tripled the contributions she

exacted from her subject states. But there is not a word of this in Thucydides. A quite extensive list could be made of matters we today see as relevant to the war that Thucydides fails to mention or about which he gives few details or to which he attaches much importance.

It is clear, therefore, what Thucydides' history is not. It is not a history of Athens or Sparta from 431 to 411, much less a history of Greece during this period. It is not even, strictly speaking, a history of the war generally conceived. The special focus Thucydides takes is announced in the second sentence: "This was the greatest *kinêsis* in Greek history." The word means disturbance or upheaval. Thucydides is concerned with the disruptive and destructive effects that the war had on Greece, both materially and psychologically. Historical factors that are regular and abiding—whether in politics, culture, the economy or society—are not set forth in any systematic way, since they are not symptoms of *kinêsis*. But when war disrupts what is normal and enduring, Thucydides' attention is immediately engaged. His work has been dubbed a disaster narrative, and with reason, for it aims to highlight the breakdown in ethics and morale as the norms of civilized life give way under the pressures of all-out war. "War is a violent teacher," he says (3.82), by which he means that war is violent in itself and is the teacher of violence.

In addition to his severe selectivity and narrow focus, Thucydides differs from Herodotus in another important respect. The older historian frequently informs us of the conflicting versions of his sources. We can see some of the dilemmas he faced in choosing among them and the criteria he adopted when judging their worth. Occasionally he will confess to personal doubts as to the truth of a fact or story. At other times he will leave the reader to decide what to believe, casting himself in the role of reporter. Thucydides' method is far different. He remarks in Book 1:

> In reference to the narrative of events in the war, I did not think it right to base it on information that chanced to come my way or on personal impressions; instead, I have investigated with as much accuracy as possible each particular involved in the events I witnessed myself and learned of from others. This was not an easy task because those present at the same event did not agree among themselves, but spoke as favoritism or imperfect memory prompted.
>
> (1.22)

What Thucydides presents are the conclusions he reached. He scarcely ever identifies his sources or specifies points on which they agreed or disagreed; nor does he set forth the criteria he used to judge the truth or express any doubts he may have had (a passage like 7.44 is unusual). In fact, he never uses the word *historía* or its cognates to describe his activity as a historian; instead, he is fond of the rather colorless verb *xyngraphô* (e.g. 1.1, 6.7), meaning to report. It is a word associated with technical prose treatises and suggests not the process of inquiry but the finished product. The result is that Thucydides presents us with the facade of an edifice so completely finished that we can only guess upon what foundation it rests and what the interior framing is that supports the exterior we see. Nevertheless, some bits of information from other sources do survive that enable us to check his accuracy, and it is to his credit that there are few points on which he can be shown to have been in error and a great many on which he has been proved correct.

Just before speaking of the diligence required to produce an accurate narrative of events at 1.22, Thucydides states his policy on the speeches in his history:

> As for the speeches each side made either in preparing to go to war or during it, it has been difficult for me to remember accurately what was said in regard to those I heard myself and those reported to me from other sources. I have given the speeches as I thought each person or group said what was required on different occasions, keeping as close as possible to the overall sense of what was actually said.

The meaning of this passage has been endlessly discussed, especially the last sentence, and with reason. He cannot mean that he wrote the speeches as *he* thought would have best suited the speakers and occasions, for in that case he need not have bothered to keep "as close as possible to the general sense of what was actually said." So the speeches are to a degree objective. But to what degree? Does what I have translated as "overall sense" (*xumpasês gnômês*) mean a capsule summary that might consist of a few lines or a fuller summary of individual points and arguments? Or did his practice vary, depending on how much information on each speech was available? Surely the latter point must have been a factor, although we cannot be sure how it may have applied to particular speeches. On the other hand, Thucydides' use of the adjective *xumpasês* elsewhere in his history, which I have translated "overall," suggests that he means something brief; one scholar renders the phrase as "main thesis," restricting it to what could

71

be said in a single sentence or so. It must be remembered that in historical writing a speech was far more detailed than any narrative episode: word follows word, argument follows argument in a period of seconds or moments. No event was ever so minutely recounted. Hence greater accuracy was possible in narrating events; Thucydides singles out favoritism for one side or the other, in addition to faulty or partial memory, as the chief obstacle to accuracy. But in speeches, he cites memory alone as the stumbling block; and it was a great one—even, as he confesses, in the case of speeches he heard himself.

Although he kept as close as he could to what was actually said, much of what is in the speeches is necessarily Thucydidean. Obviously this is true of the language. It is also true for selectivity: Thucydides does not say or imply that he reproduced all the points he knew a speaker made on a particular occasion. It is also true of shape and emphasis. Thucydides surely highlighted those issues and arguments that he considered the most significant. In the end, the speeches are a blend of what was actually said and of what Thucydides himself thought were the most important issues, both explicit and implicit, underlying the position each speaker argued.

Something must also be said of Thucydides' style and authorial stance. His Greek favors archaisms and poetic coloring, as well as inconcinnity and dislocation of normal word order; concision and rapidity are also characteristic. The language is frequently difficult, the speeches especially so; even the ancients found them heavy going, employing as they do frequent abstractions and arresting coinages. Antithesis is the most characteristic feature of the writing. While the structure of Greek encourages the balancing of opposed ideas, with, for example, its pervasive *men . . . de* construction ("on the one hand . . . on the other"), in Thucydides the juxtaposition of opposites is found at every level, from phrases, clauses and sentences to whole speeches and narrative patterns. The speeches are especially striking in this regard. They often appear in opposing pairs, as in the first book when the Corcyreans argue for and the Corinthians against Athens allying with Corcyra (1.32–36; 37–43), or the Corinthians condemn Athens and urge Sparta to go to war while the Athenians defend the acquisition of their empire (1.68–71; 73–78), which is followed immediately by the Spartan king Archidamus speaking against going to war and the ephor Sthenelaidas arguing tersely in favor (1.80–85; 86). Speeches may answer one another even when not given on the same occasion: Pericles' first speech at Athens urging the people to go to war (1.140–144) is in some parts a point-by-point riposte to what the

Corinthians had said earlier in Sparta (1.68–71). Even Pericles' last speech (2.60–64) corrects or amplifies certain points he made in his funeral oration some chapters before (2.35–46).

The penchant for arguing persuasively on the opposite sides of a question, which was especially characteristic of sophistic teaching, finds its analogue in the narrative. The paired portraits of Pausanias and Themistocles at the end of Book 1 comprise one example (128–134; 135–138). And both narrative and speech can be woven into a complex web of antitheses that extend over large stretches of the text. The juxtaposed fates of the two towns of Mitylene and Plataea, covering three-quarters of Book 3 (1–86), are illustrative. The first concerns Mitylene (3.1–50; to be discussed shortly in greater detail), an ally of Athens which had revolted and had appealed for Spartan help to prevent recapture, but which in the end was forced to capitulate. Mitylene's fate was twice debated in the Athenian assembly; Thucydides reproduces the two speeches from the second meeting that "were most in opposition to one another" (3.49). In the end, she was saved from annihilation by a last-minute change of heart on the part of the Athenians. The case of Plataea follows immediately (3.41–86). The town was a staunch ally of Athens, despite its inland situation in Boeotia next to Attica. After a successful siege, the Spartans held a trial of those who had surrendered. The Plataeans in a speech urge mercy (3.53–59); their neighbors, the Thebans, argue for punishment (3.61–67). Sparta responded by bringing the Plataeans in singly and asking each what service he had done Sparta or her allies in the present war. When they admitted they had given none, all were executed to a man; the women were enslaved (3.68). Sparta wanted to preserve the appearance of correctness in staging a "trial;" but the verdict she reached was aimed at pleasing the Thebans, "whom she thought would prove useful in a war that was in its beginning phase."

The reader thus is continually being presented with opposing speeches and contrasting narrative episodes. It is a challenging and difficult style, since resolution and authorial comment are seldom presented. The reader is left to perceive for him or herself the significance of the various arguments put forward in the speeches and the implications of juxtapositions in the narrative. Yet Thucydides controls his subject matter with a sure hand and is supremely confident in his selection of material and in his rare authorial pronouncements. His self-assurance cannot fail to impress, and is at times almost intimidating. His persona contrasts strongly with that of Herodotus, who appears at first sight as a talkative and

73

engaging raconteur, somewhat childlike in his curiosity and guileless candor. The two authors are excellent examples of how strongly self-presentation colors one's estimate of a writer. In Herodotus' case judgments have frequently been indulgently patronizing, in Thucydides' almost reverential. Both are extreme and unjustified. Yet in Thucydides' case one must admit that, like the Ancient Mariner, he "hath his will" and we, his listeners, "cannot choose but hear."

There is a significant exception to Thucydides' practice of not disclosing his sources or his methods of evaluating them. This occurs in chapters 1–23 of the opening book, the *Archaeology*. It is not typical of what follows because here Thucydides' subject is early Greek history, his purpose being to review past conflicts and compare them in magnitude and duration with the Peloponnesian War. In order to ascertain the truth about conditions and events in old Greece, he openly discusses what evidence he finds trustworthy and why he makes the deductions he does.

Since he accepts the basic historicity of the Trojan War and even of a personage like Minos of Crete (1.4, 8), he feels entitled to use the evidence of Homer and other early poets in making his arguments. For example, he wants to know, as Herodotus had, why the Trojan War lasted ten years. Herodotus, having argued that Helen was in Egypt throughout the war (2.120), was at a loss to explain the refusal of the Greeks to believe the Trojans when they kept saying they did not have her. The gods, he concludes, must have blinded the Greeks to the truth in order to demonstrate to mankind that great misdeeds are severely punished. Thucydides argues that Agamemnon's large force was not served by supply routes and hence was obliged to engage in agriculture and piracy in order to sustain itself. It was therefore not able to concentrate its power together at any one time: if it had done so, the war would have been over much quicker (1.11).

Yet Thucydides is well aware that information about the distant past was uncertain (1.1, 21; cf. 6.2). The very fact that much of it derived from the poets made it suspect: Homer was born long after the Trojan War he wrote about (1.3) and, as a poet, was likely to exaggerate (1.10). But Thucydides believes he can still use the testimony of the poets: first, because for him the Trojan War was a real war involving real people, and second, because he is able to test some of what the poets had to say by appealing to conditions of his own day. For example, he finds them describing customs that still survived in backward areas of contemporary Greece; he deduces from this that in earlier days these customs were prevalent throughout Greece: for example, the habit of always going armed—both to engage in brigandage and to defend against it—or the siting of cities away from the coastline to thwart piracy (1.5–7). Thucydides also adduces purely archaeological evidence. Graves dug up on the island of Delos revealed them to be Carian in the manner of burial and the weapons they contained: hence he identifies the Carians as early colonists of the Aegean islands who made their mark by successful pirateering (1.8). On the other hand, he realizes that physical remains may deceive. The town of Sparta was a collection of villages without large or impressive public buildings, a condition typical of old Greece; if all that were left was the physical site, one would never realize what Sparta's true power had been. The reverse is true of Athens: if her population suddenly disappeared, the material remains would make her power seem twice as great as it actually was.

Thucydides' main focus in the *Archaeology* is on the question of what constitutes power in Greek history, by which he means the ability of states to build empires and undertake other great enterprises, especially wars. As he reviews this question from the time of Minos to the present day, he finds three indispensable conditions: such a state must dominate the sea, it must have subject allies and it must have money. The extent to which a state possesses these prerequisites will determine the degree of its success. Thucydides clearly has taken Athens' empire as the yardstick by which to measure the success of earlier enterprises. This is partly because, as he looks back on earlier periods, those that were impressive—Minos in Crete, Agamemnon's expedition to Troy, Corinth's rise to power, for example—all were based on navies, dependent allies and wealth. No land-based state in mainland Greece had ever succeeded as the naval powers had done. He makes an exception of some of the Greek tyrants in Sicily (1.17); he does not consider foreign land empires, such as that of Persia.

All in all, the *Archaeology* is an impressive piece of analysis, strikingly modern in many of its methods. His evaluation of written evidence is remarkable, for he endeavors wherever possible to check it by material evidence, by analogy with practices in contemporary Greece, as well as by appealing to probability and internal consistency. Equally impressive are his results. It may be somewhat of a distortion to take Athens' empire as the standard by which to judge the success of earlier enterprises; nevertheless, control of the sea and the acquisition of tribute-paying subject states were indeed what led to wealth and power, at least in Greek history up to his day. As for the rest, he seems correct in most of his main conclusions, among them the disunity and more primitive way of life in early Greece, and that the Peloponnesian War far surpassed all earlier conflicts in intensity, destruction and duration.

Comparison of Thucydides' version of the war with standard modern accounts shows that episodes to which he devoted many pages often receive only a paragraph or two, if that, in modern treatments. One reason for this is that the narrative–speech format of ancient historiography encouraged the circumstantial recounting of words and actions. Yet in the hands of a master like Thucydides the format also permits the writer to bring out points of major significance in seemingly minor events.

An example is his account of the revolt of Mitylene at 3.1–50, which takes up two-fifths of the book. Mitylene was the chief city of the island of Lesbos, one of the more important member states of Athens' empire. In the fourth year of the war (428 BC) she, along with all the cities on the island save one, revolted. Spartan support was sought and granted, but before help arrived Mitylene capitulated to the blockading Athenians. Lesbos was one of only two states that contributed ships and crews to Athens; she was not liable to exactions of tribute. The Athenians, enraged that a member enjoying "favored nation" status would revolt, voted that the women and children be enslaved and all the adult males be put to death (3.36). A ship was sent to carry the grim news. But overnight many Athenians had a revulsion of feeling and on the next day, after vigorous debate, rescinded in a close vote the previous day's decision. Another ship was dispatched, which managed to arrive just before the sentence of execution was to be carried out. "Mitylene had a close call," Thucydides dryly remarks (3.49).

On the surface the Mitylenian affair does not appear particularly important: a revolt is quickly put down, the punishment for which is amended in an overnight change of heart; conditions revert pretty much to what they had been before. Yet Thucydides sees encapsulated in the episode many of the pivotal issues of the war, and this is why he describes it in such detail. One is the justification for Mitylene's action that Thucydides puts in the mouths of the envoys sent to win Spartan support (3.9–14). In arguing for the rightness of her cause, Mitylene lays bare the plight and psychology of Athens' subjects at large: "We did not become allies of the Athenians to enslave the Greeks but allies of the Greeks to free them from the Persians" (3.10). Furthermore, the "favored" status was a sham because Athens would revoke it when it

76

suited her: her ever-increasing power would not permit her to countenance the ostensible independence of a lesser state for very long (3.11), a sentiment which the Athenians themselves admit to at a later stage of the war: the independence of even a weak neutral set a bad example for everyone, she was to say (5.95: the Melian Dialogue). Moreover, the Mitylenian envoys continue, if the Spartans think that far-off Lesbos is not a factor in the war, they are mistaken: "The war will not be decided in Attica, as some imagine, but in those states by which Attica is sustained. Her allies are the source of her revenue, which will become even greater if we succumb" (3.13).

Another significant factor is the response of Sparta and her allies. The latter were slow to answer the call for immediate help because the harvest was upon them and they were tired of so much military service (3.15). Sparta did not dispatch a fleet to aid the blockaded Mitylenians until the following summer; yet despite the late start, the forty-nine ships proved so dilatory in their progress across the Aegean that the city, despairing of their arrival, capitulated to the besieging Athenians. Two proposals were then made to the Spartan admiral Alcidas, both of which he rejected. One was to come at once to Mitylene's rescue, taking the Athenians by surprise (3.29–30). The other was to seize one of the cities of Ionia subject to Athens, thereby creating a base to foster revolts throughout Ionia: Athens would be deprived of her greatest source of revenue and it would cost her much expense to mount a counterattack. "This was a feasible proposal," Thucydides observes, "for the Spartans were welcomed everywhere they went" (3.31). Alcidas was instead so anxious to be back in the Peloponnesus that he went straight back across the open sea, fearful that he might be spotted and have to confront the Athenian fleet.

This aspect of the episode admirably mirrors the national characters of the two protagonists as the Corinthians describe them when urging Sparta to go to war in the opening book (1.70–71). The Athenians, they say, are ever ready to try something new and to act the aggressors, quickly planning and executing whatever they set their minds on.

> They do not hesitate to act, you procrastinate. They are never at home, you are ever there. For they think that by being away they will add to their possessions, you that by going afield you may jeopardize what you have.... In short, one would be right to say that by nature they take no rest themselves and give none to others.
>
> (1.70)

The Spartans, the Corinthians continue, are the opposite: preoccupied with preserving what they have, they stick to their old ways and are reluctant to act; and when they do, they take half measures. There is doubtless some degree of exaggeration in what the Corinthians say, but not much: Thucydides' comments at 4.55 and 8.96 show that this was his judgment of the two states as well. Hence Alcidas' character neatly replicates that of his countrymen generally, and points up one of Sparta's major weaknesses.

The episode also confirms the Corinthians' description of the Athenian character in one telling particular. The Mitylenians argue that the devastating effects of the plague on Athens and the great expense she has incurred so far in the war have created the perfect moment for Sparta to act: it is unlikely, they maintain, that Athens can make an effective response, given the present commitments of her fleet (3.13). But the Mitylenians misjudged Athens: determined not to betray weakness, she immediately fitted out one hundred new ships and sent them to ravage the Peloponnesian coastline, utterly deflating Sparta's expectations (3.16). It was a swift and daring move that stretched Athens' capabilities considerably.

The Mitylenian affair illustrates another fundamental truth of the Peloponnesian War: the changeableness of the Athenian populace as it is swayed by emotion and by the competing rhetoric of rival political leaders. Thucydides reproduces a full-scale exchange between the two men who gave the most opposed opinions when the assembly met to reconsider its vote of the day before (3.37–48). On the one side is Cleon, "the most violent man in Athens" (3.36), on the other Diodotus, known to history only here. Both men make dark insinuations about speakers who out of questionable motives try to win popularity by clever rhetoric and fair-sounding arguments. Cleon in particular castigates his audience for their fondness for the "pleasures of the ear" (3.38) and opens his speech by saying (3.37): "Past experience has taught me that a democracy is incapable of empire, and I am particularly convinced of this truth now, when I see your change of heart in the matter of Mitylene." Cleon argues for adhering to their vote of the day before; weakness in dealing with the rebels will only encourage others to revolt: "You do not see that your empire is a tyranny and that you rule over unwilling subjects who would conspire against you" (3.37). It is both just and expedient to punish the Mitylenians, he concludes; Athens must not succumb to "the three greatest threats to empire: pity, sentiment and softness" (3.40). Diodotus' responds by saying that the question before them is not the guilt of the Mitylenians, but what best serves the interests of Athens' empire. Capital punishment is an ineffective deterrent to those who are desperate and daring: "Either some more terrible deterrent must be found or it must be accounted useless" (3.45). Moreover, to enslave and kill the whole population, rather than punish the ringleaders of the revolt, will cause disaffection among the mass of people in the democratic cities of Athens' empire (3.47).

Diodotus concludes by saying that despite his opposition to Cleon there is one point on which they both agree: the Athenians must not cast their votes out of pity or softness, but according to what will best serve the interests of Athens' empire. The vote is close, but Diodotus prevails. The irony is that the people vote not on the basis of the arguments presented to them but from the one motive that both speakers agree should have no influence; for that pity was the prime factor in their change of heart Thucydides makes clear even before the debate begins (3.36).

Many other examples of this technique, which might ponderously be dubbed "history by synecdoche," can be found in Thucydides: an episode and its details are made to represent abiding issues in the historical picture overall. Rather than giving generalized analyses of issues, conditions, institutions and the like, as is the norm in modern histories, the ancient historians—or at least the better ones—most often exemplify such issues as these through speeches and the narration of concrete events; their deeper meaning the perceptive reader is left to deduce for him or herself. Rarely Thucydides is explicit about this method. In commenting on the factional strife that engulfed Corcyra (to be discussed in the next chapter), he stresses that this was one of the first instances of what was to become endemic as the war tightened its grip on the Greek world (3.82, 84–85): what he describes now, he says, will be representative of all the internal revolutions that followed. Yet what happened to Corcyra is made to represent much more. Thucydides' description of the Corcyrean revolution and his extensive meditation on its causes go to the heart of what the war was about generally and instruct us not just about Greek factionalism, but human nature itself.

79

5

THUCYDIDES
Science and tragedy

Thucydides alone of the ancient historians has received the accolade "scientific" from the moderns. For some he has been the exemplar par excellence: his intellectual rigor, meticulous deployment of evidence and accuracy have seemed to many a model of what serious history should aim to be in all ages. Yet there have been some sharp dissenters. He was a literary artist, these critics reply, bent on shaping his material to achieve the effects of Greek tragedy: the reader becomes a spectator of the action and feels pity and fear as the drama unfolds. In short, his appeal was more to art than to science, more to emotion than to intellect. Still others have emphasized the element of chance and accident over and above the claims of intelligence and reason. Thus a great tug of war has been waged, and is still being waged, between utterly opposed interpretations: science versus art, intellect versus emotion, the predictable versus the accidental, the rational versus the irrational. It is the aim of this chapter to discuss the persuasiveness of these different views.

For a long time, especially in the nineteenth century and the first part of the twentieth, serious students believed that when history was correctly done it deserved to be styled a science: that is, it was an objective endeavor to discover the truth, and was carried out by an exacting deployment of data from which ineluctable conclusions were deduced. Few people now believe in this scientific model, which seems in this latter day utopian. The realization that the historian is a prisoner of his own milieu, tied to the values and perspective of the age in which he lives, makes the attainment of pure, objective truth seem impossible. Moreover, history is not now generally viewed as enjoying an independent existence awaiting discovery, but is the creation of the historian, each historian having a somewhat different agenda and different perspective from all others.

So the notion of Thucydides being a scientific historian, as science has sometimes been understood, has been largely shunted aside, if not discarded, albeit reluctantly in some quarters. On the other hand, the influence of *ancient* science on Thucydides is undeniable: I refer specifically to medical science as we see it described in a few late fifth-century treatises that have come down to us, along with others, under the name of Hippocrates of Cos, the father of medicine. Very little is known of Hippocrates himself, and none of the treatises can be ascribed to him, although some are certainly by his followers. And although it is difficult, if not impossible, to formulate a coherent theory of medicine for the early Hippocratic school, those treatises of the Hippocratic corpus that date to the fifth century exhibit certain attitudes and methods that are sharply relevant to Thucydides. First, these physicians regarded medicine as a *technê*: that is, as a specialized field of study using methods and principles peculiar to itself and capable of reaching secure results. They repudiated the type of medicine that was largely based on preconceived philosophical postulates, such as that the body, like the rest of the physical world, was composed of the hot, the cold, the wet and the dry and that diseases resulted from an imbalance among these qualities. Instead, they believed that the causes of disease were multiple and complex, and were to be deduced by close observation and the compilation of many case studies. Only then could the various diseases be distinguished from one another and treatment appropriate to each undertaken.

Medicine was therefore investigative by nature; the word *historía* and its cognates are frequently used to describe the course pursued by the doctor and the close observation required of him. One of the principal aims of these early physicians was classification; when a particular disease could be distinguished from others, *diagnôsis* (literally, means of distinguishing) was possible. Moreover, classification was universally applicable: causes and symptoms were everywhere the same in the world. Once the doctor had identified a particular disease in a patient, it was especially important to anticipate the *krisis*, that decisive day or days on which the physician must use all his skills to bring the patient through; if the patient survived the *krisis* stage, recovery was likely. Identification of a disease and selection of appropriate treatment depended on two key factors: first, knowledge gained from past experience of many patients both by himself and other physicians (one of the treatises in the Hippocratic corpus contains forty-two such case studies from a doctor's daily notebook); second, close examination of the patient and his environment (such as season of year, climate, geographical situation, quality of the local water) and asking him to speak about his past medical history and current symptoms, both physical and mental.

The physician's goal was *prognôsis*, inference in advance. *Prognôsis* depended on combining what the doctor knew about a disease generally and what variables peculiar to patient and environment he was able to discover. *Prognôsis* involved, therefore, proceeding from the seen to the unseen, from the observed to what was hidden from sight. The physician was trying to understand what was going on inside the body; relying on his inferences, he would be able to anticipate what course the disease was likely to take in the coming days. Moreover, divine explanations for diseases, while admitted as a factor, should not, these Hippocratic writers believed, be the sole or even chief concern of the doctor. Epilepsy, for example, which was called the sacred disease because it was popularly believed that a spirit took possession of the body, was declared by one medical writer to be no more divine than any other:

> This disease does not seem to me more divine than other diseases, but has its own nature [*physis*] as other diseases do, and its own visible warning signs [*prophasis*], as each of the others have. And it is curable, no less than others are.
>
> (*The Sacred Disease* 5)

That Hippocratic medical science had a direct influence on Thucydides can be seen in his detailed description of the plague that broke out in Athens in 430 BC and continued for several years (2.47–54). A quarter of the population perished, including Pericles. The historian, who caught the disease but survived, therefore says he speaks from personal experience and from close observation of fellow victims (2.48). If someone happened to be suffering from a prior malady, it invariably turned into the plague, while those in excellent health were struck down suddenly without any visible warning signs (*prophasis*) of what was to come (2.49). The doctors were baffled because at first they did not know how to treat the disease, while proving particularly susceptible themselves in their constant attendance upon the sick (2.46). Thucydides therefore gives a careful description of all general symptoms "in order that it may be recognized again, should it recur" (2.48). He is careful to note the *krisis*, which he fixes on the sixth and eighth days, when most fatalities occurred. Of those who survived the eighth day, many succumbed later when the disease invaded the bowels (2.49). He also stresses the varied psychological reactions: panic, selfless attendance upon friends and family, religious hysteria and the breakdown of normal modes of civilized behavior.

Another telling indication of the influence of medical science on the historian is the word *prophasis*, whose usual meaning in Greek is alleged reason or justification, whether true or false. Thucydides most often uses it in this sense; for example, after Sparta and her allies had resolved on war, both they and Athens proceeded to charge one another with being under a religious curse in order to have "a powerful pretext" (*megistê prophasis*, 1.126) for engaging in hostilities. On the other hand, in the medical writers the word regularly means those visible signs that point to the coming of a full-blown disease. We thus are faced with an ambiguity that is perplexing, if not perverse: the same word ostensibly means both the verbal justification given for one's conduct (subjective) and the visible signs pointing to conditions that are yet to develop (objective). But two etymologies lie behind the homonyms: the first derives from the word to say (*pha-* from *phêmi*), the second from *phainomai*, meaning be evident. Through the fifth century the second usage is quite uncommon outside the medical writers. Thucydides pointedly takes it over. One clear example comes in the description of the plague: those in excellent health suddenly fell ill "without any visible warning signs" (2.49).

But Thucydides extends the medical meaning of *prophasis* further in two crucial passages. At the conclusion of the *Archaeology* and as he is about to relate the incidents at Corcyra and Potidaea (which he terms *aitiai*, or grounds of complaint), he writes a passage that plays on two root words: *pha-* from *phainomai* and *leg-*, to say (or its noun *log-*, speech):

> As to why they broke it [the peace treaty], I put first the grounds of complaint and points of dispute so that no one may ever search out the source of such a war among the Greeks. For I consider the truest cause [*alêthestatê prophasis*], which was the one least evident in speech [*aphanestatê de logôi*], to be the fact that Athens' growing power and the fear that this caused Sparta forced them into war. The grounds of complaint spoken by both sides as evidence [*es to phaneron legomenai*] were as follows . . .
>
> (1.23)

The narrative concerning Corcyra is thus launched. Thucydides marks the unique meaning he gives the word *prophasis* here in several ways: by contrasting it with *aitiai*, or spoken grounds of complaint, by using the adjective "truest" as a modifier and by paradoxical wordplay. The truest "evident cause" is that which was "least evident" in speech, whereas the grounds of complaint were those "spoken in evidence." The second appearance of the phrase *alêthestatê prophasis* (and its last appearance in all of Greek) comes when Thucydides is preparing to begin his narrative of the Sicilian expedition (6.6): the "truest cause" was Athens' desire to conquer the whole island, which the historian contrasts with Athens' avowed motive of coming to the aid of those related to her and of their allies. I have translated *alêthestatê prophasis* in these two passages as "cause." Both involve states of mind: Sparta's fear of Athens' growing power in 1.23 and Athens' unstated desire to conquer all of Sicily at 6.6. Both can be seen as "preliminary signs" of what was to come in the medical sense; but here they are far from being "visible," since they are motives that Sparta in the first instance and Athens in the second refused to voice aloud. Rather than being the outward manifestation of the cause we cannot see, *prophasis* here denotes a true, or efficient, cause.

After identifying a disease, the doctor aimed to anticipate the stages through which it would pass: *prognôsis*. Competent ministration to the patient depended on such "inference in advance." Similarly, in Thucydides' eyes the ability to predict intelligently the course of future events constituted the chief merit of great statesmen and of the study of history generally. Whether Thucydides took this idea from medicine in particular is debatable, but it seems plausible. The historian frankly admires Pericles for many qualities, but praises especially his prescience: he correctly estimated the greatness of Athens' power in the coming struggle and foresaw that Athens would win easily if she followed his advice to stay quiet, to maintain the fleet and to take no unnecessary risks (2.65: Thucydides twice uses the verb from which *prognôsis* derives). The same predictive ability is also singled out as Themistocles' most outstanding quality (1.138): "he was the best at divining the future, having the surest grasp of what was actually to come about."

Thucydides claims the same predictive intelligence for history. In fact, he claims it for himself in his opening sentence when he asserts that he foresaw at the outbreak of the war how great and important it would be, in consequence of which he began preparation for writing at once. At 1.22 he delivers a programmatic statement on the nature and value of history, part of which has been quoted earlier:

> Possibly the absence of the story-telling element in my history may make it less entertaining. But I will be satisfied if those people judge my history useful who desire an accurate picture of past events and those to come, which, given man's nature, will recur from time to time in a similar or analogous fashion. My work is a possession for all time, not a showpiece designed to catch the applause of the moment.

Thucydides does not explain in this statement just what sort of recurring events he has in mind. It has been argued that he refers here to events future to himself, not to his reader: his history will enable them to understand events that have already happened or are in the course of happening, but not to anticipate what is yet to come. Yet the exclusion of a predictive value to history is unwarranted. Other passages suggest he has, at least in part, just this value in mind. The most important of these come in his discussion of the internal revolution at Corcyra (3.82–84), which entailed frightful savagery as each political faction violated the norms of civilized behavior to achieve its ends, all the while cloaking its behavior under fair-sounding names such as patriotism and honor. The clash between the democratic party that favored Athens and the oligarchs who supported Sparta recurred thereafter in many cities throughout the Greek world:

> The calamities that befell these cities because of the factionalism were many and terrible, such as have occurred and always will occur as long as man's nature remains the same, becoming severer or milder and taking different forms as circumstances change.
>
> (3.82)

A bit later he reverts to the same theme (some, however, question the authenticity of this section):

> As life in the city was now thrown into confusion (*xuntar-achthentos*), human nature, predisposed to flout the laws (*nomoi*), gladly showed itself to be uncontrollable in its fury, the subverter of justice, hostile to everything its superior. . . . When bent on vengeance, men think it right to do away with those general laws (*nomoi*) designed to protect all men in adversity and

85

not to let them remain in force to a time when danger threatens and they will need them.

(3.84)

The key to understanding these passages lies, I believe, in Thucydides' concept of human nature, variously expressed as *to anthrôpinon* (1.22), *physis anthrôpôn* (3.82) and *anthrôpeia physis* (3.84). *Physis* in Greek denotes an ever-present characteristic that is inherent in a thing, wherever it is in the world. It is opposed to those artificial constraints that man has created to ensure an ordered society, which the Greeks called *nomoi* (sing. *nomos*) and I have translated as laws, but which can also refer to customs and habits. *Nomoi* are relative, therefore, varying from people to people and city to city. Thucydides' remarks here fit into the debate among philosophers and sophists in the late fifth century generally as to the rival claims of *nomos* and *physis*: the real nature of each and which plays, or should play, the more fundamental role in man's life. Thucydides makes his own view of man's *physis* abundantly clear: it is part of his nature and prompts him as an individual or as a member of a group to break the laws if he can get away with it, in an effort to secure what he regards as his own best interests. Laws are designed to protect all citizens equally, especially in times of great crisis (compare Pericles' remarks in his funeral speech, 2.37); the terrible irony is that the laws often fail society at just those moments when people most need their protection.

Man's *physis*, because it is constant and abiding in all men everywhere, is probably the most significant reason why some future events will be similar to those in the past. It emerges into full view at moments when men feel their lives and security threatened, as in a plague or a war. When Thucydides describes the plague that descended on Athens in 430 BC, he devotes as much space to its psychological as to its physical effects. The number of people in the city had greatly increased by the influx of the country people of Attica, who because of Spartan invasions of Attica were forced to live in makeshift shelters, mostly within the Long Walls. As the bodies of the dead and dying piled up in temples and other public places, the regular customs of burial (*nomoi*, 2.52) were thrown into confusion (*xunetarachthêsan*). The absence of law was the result (*a-nomia*, 2.53): neither fear of the gods nor the law of men (*anthrôpôn nomos*) deterred people from living for the pleasures of the moment, as they unexpectedly succeeded to the property of those who had died: they thought they would soon succumb to the disease

86

themselves and did not expect to be brought to account for their offenses.

Behavior such as occurred during the plague and on Corcyra is doubtless what Thucydides chiefly has in mind when he refers to those future events "which, given man's nature, will recur from time to time in a similar or analogous fashion" (1.22). Hence, history is not cyclical. The adverb I have translated "from time to time" (*pote*) refers to indefinite points in the future. What can be anticipated is the emergence of man's *physis* when provoked by great calamities. Yet calamities like plagues and wars occur irregularly, and some of them, such as plagues, can scarcely be anticipated in advance. Nor will man's *physis* express itself in the same way on each occasion, but will take different forms depending on circumstances. So the predictive lesson of history refers to a general wisdom rather than to knowledge of specifics. Prudent men will anticipate such general reactions and will be prepared for them. Thus Pericles foresaw the response of the Athenians to the devastation by the Peloponnesians of Attic territory. After the second invasion in 430 BC they became dispirited; the outbreak of the plague in the same year caused outright despair. They vented their anger on Pericles and even sent ambassadors to Sparta, who made an unsuccessful attempt to sue for peace. Pericles had anticipated this general reaction, says Thucydides (2.59), who reports a lengthy speech the statesman made designed to firm up their resolve (2.60–64), in the course of which he asserts that of their misfortunes only the plague was not foreseen (2.64); all the rest he had anticipated, both that the Spartans would invade and how the Athenians would respond to it.

In the last chapter it was argued that Thucydides' chief focus in his history was not upon Greece during the twenty-seven-year period of the war nor even upon the war generally conceived, but on the war as disturbance or upheaval: *kinêsis* (1.1). The analogy with medicine is striking, though perhaps accidental. Just as the doctor's attention is fixed on abnormalities and traumas inflicted by disease upon the healthy body, so Thucydides concentrates on the disastrous effect war had on the body politic of Greece, particularly its psychological effects. Moreover, the narrative–speech format, though derived from Homer through Herodotus, is much like the two chief sources of information that the physician uses: a detailed record of the outward symptoms of a disease and the statements of the patient concerning his past medical history and present feelings. Reading the speeches in Thucydides as if they were reports by patients can be helpful and illuminating: the listener takes the statements seriously, because they contain essential information. But they are only a part of a complex syndrome whose true nature must be pieced together from many different sources. The doctor and historian aim to discover "the truest cause" that lies hidden beneath the surface of what they see and hear, which is also the task of the intelligent reader.

From the few comments Thucydides makes in his own person, such as those at 1.22, 3.82 and 3.84, his view of human nature emerges. But embedded in the many speeches he assigns to parties in the conflict are comments on a somewhat different aspect of man's *physis*, in which the stronger are described as dominating the weak by an immutable law of nature, and which is characterized as more powerful than law or custom, and irresistible once it is roused. Diodotus in the Mitylenian debate, for example, asserts:

> All men by nature do wrong, both individuals and states, and no law (*nomos*) exists that can stop it.... In short, it is impossible and utterly foolish for anyone to think that once human nature (*anthrôpeia physis*) is bent on doing something it can be dissuaded by the force of law (*nomos*) or some other deterrent.
>
> (3.45)

This impulse in man is most frequently cited in the speeches of Athenians attempting to explain or justify their empire. Thus the Athenian spokesmen who chanced to be in Sparta when the Peloponnesian League was debating whether to go to war say this:

> We did nothing surprising or contrary to the way men behave if we accepted an empire when it was offered to us and do not now give it up under the compelling constraints of prestige, fear and self-interest. We were not the first to do this, but it has always been the case that the weaker is subject to the stronger. We thought we were worthy of empire, and so we seemed to you until now, when calculation of expediency has led you to adopt an argument from justice, which has never yet deterred anyone from realizing his ambition when there was a chance of getting something by force. The ones who are worthy of praise are those who, while following the dictates of human nature (*anthrôpeia physis*), show themselves to be more just in ruling others than their power requires.
>
> (1.76)

This frank appraisal finds even more naked expression
Athenians decide in 415 BC to annex the neutral island
which had the misfortune to be in a strategic location and to
model of independence to the subject states in Athens' en...
three motives for empire—prestige, fear and self-interest, dubbed the
"unholy trinity" of Athenian imperialism—are clearly brought out in
the dialogue: Melos' independence causes Athens' reputation to suffer
since it is a sign of weakness to her subjects (5.95); she consequently
fears the overthrow of her empire by those she rules (5.91, 97); it is in
her self-interest to preserve and foster her empire (5.91). Furthermore:

> Of divinity we believe and of mankind we are positive that by
> constraint of nature (*physis*) each rules those over whom it has
> power. We did not invent this behavior (*nomos*), nor were we the
> first to act on it, but we act on something that was already
> existing when we took it up and will continue to exist after we
> lay it down, and we know that you and others would do likewise
> if you possessed the same power.
>
> (5.105)

On one occasion even a potential victim of Athenian imperialism
agrees with this view. Hermocrates of Syracuse in reference to Athens'
designs on Sicily says:

> It is completely excusable for the Athenians to seek to expand
> and to look out for their interests. I fault not those who want to
> rule, but those who are ready to knuckle under. For it has always
> been as much a part of man's nature to protect himself against
> aggression as it is to rule those who give in to him.
>
> (4.61)

Such appeals to man's nature should not be regarded as rhetorical
ploys designed to explain or justify aggression. Rather, they appear as
a strongly felt belief on the part of many people; we see this in much of
late fifth-century literature—sophists, dramatists and orators—and
championed early in the next century by some of Plato's more
combative interlocutors, such as Callicles in the *Gorgias* and
Thrasymachus in the *Republic*. Many people, therefore, believed that
this was the way the world worked: the strong ruled where they could
and the weak suffered what they must (cf. 5.89, 6.85). It was not a
matter of might makes right, but was simply a harsh fact of existence.
But did Thucydides believe it? For it must not be assumed that he
subscribed to the views advanced by the speakers in his history, even a

view that is repeatedly expressed, as this is. Decision is not easy. But I am inclined to think that the historian did so view human nature. The basic thrust of his comments on the revolution at Corcyra is that under the pressure of war man seeks to overpower his adversaries by any means he can (3.82): "The cause of all this [lawlessness] was power fueled by greed and ambition, from which passions came the partisan strife of those trying to beat down their opponents." This is not the same as saying that the strong dominate the weak as a fact of nature, but it comes close. In each formulation man's *physis* leads him to commit acts of violence under the impulse of self-aggrandizement. In addition, Hermocrates says it is as much a part of man's nature to resist subjugation as it is to subjugate others, which is borne out elsewhere in the history, especially in Melos' refusal even in the face of over-whelming force to yield to Athens without a fight.

Closely allied to this view of man's *physis* are two conceptions of human behavior that are especially associated with the sophists, but which are found in many writings of the fifth and fourth centuries. The first is the argument from likelihood, which postulates that individuals and groups will behave in regular and predictable ways based on their interests, knowledge and status in life. Crudely put, man is conditioned by the culture, polity and group to which he belongs: that is, by *nomoi*. Thus, in the *Archaeology*, Thucydides finds that certain conditions in backward areas of contemporary Greece answer to those described by Homer in his epics; hence he finds it likely that these features were prevalent everywhere in old Greece (1.2–8). The argument from likelihood is everywhere present in the history, especially in the speeches. But it can produce misguided assessments when not properly used. For example, the people of Mitylene, in appealing to Sparta to support their revolt on Lesbos, assert (correctly) that Athens' navy was at that moment fully occupied; it is not likely, they say (3.13), that Athens can launch yet another fleet to counter a Spartan move to rescue the island. But the Mitylenians underestimate the aggressive, risk-taking temper of the Athenians, who, determined to show they are not weak, fit out a hundred new ships and descend on the Peloponnesus in force. This unanticipated move dashed Spartan expectations and made them distrust what the Mitylenians had said (3.16). Yet in the hands of acute observers the principle of likelihood was a powerful tool—for statesmen in estimating behavior in the present and anticipating it in the future, for historians in discovering the truth of what has happened in the past.

The second argument derives from expedience, and is based on the

90

premise that men act in their own self-interest rather than from motives of altruism or moral principles. It is often opposed to arguments based on justice and honor. This is forcefully illustrated in the first debate in the history between the Corcyreans and the Corinthians as to whether Athens should take Corcyra as an ally. The former argue mainly from the material advantages Athens will gain (1.32–36), the latter on the basis of equity, gratitude and honorable conduct (3.37–43). When the Athenian assembly first debated the issue, it was inclined to favor Corinth, but in a second meeting feelings shifted in favor of Corcyra. Thucydides says that self-interest was the deciding factor:

> At all events, it seemed that war with Sparta would soon break out, and they did not want to make a present to Corinth of Corcyra's fine navy. . . . Then, too, the island seemed conveniently placed on the shipping lane that led to Italy and Sicily.
>
> (1.44)

Another telling example, already mentioned, comes in the speech of the Athenian envoys who chanced to be in Sparta when war was being debated by the League (1.76); the Peloponnesians, they say, now desire to screen their real motive of self-interest by adopting an argument from justice, "which has never yet deterred anyone from realizing his ambition when there was a chance of getting something by force."

From what has been said about the influence of ancient science on Thucydides and of his views on human nature, it is clear he had an austere, unsentimental conception of how the world worked. Humans sometimes behave in predictable ways partly because of instincts shared by all men everywhere (*physis*) and partly because of the culture, government and society into which a particular man is born, which go to shape his beliefs and actions (*nomoi*). Such pragmatic factors as these explain to a significant extent why events occur as they do. The divine is not a causative agent, as it is in Herodotus. Thucydides has a detached, even skeptical, view of oracles (e.g. 2.54), which is not to say he necessarily disbelieved in them. He is critical of those who interpret natural phenomena like thunder, lightning and rain as omens from heaven when natural explanations are to hand, such as their occurring at a time of year when one would expect them to (see 6.70, 7.79). At the siege of Syracuse, Nicias, who was "overly addicted to superstition and such like," postponed acting for a critical "thrice nine days" because of an eclipse of the moon (7.50; cf. 7.77); compare this with 2.28, where the historian recounts a solar eclipse in naturalistic terms.

Near the start of the history (1.23) he says that earthquakes, eclipses and droughts occurred far more frequently during the war than had been previously experienced. He gives no explanation for this. His remarks here have been compared to the medical writers, who sometimes first record facts about the season of year, weather conditions and quality of water. Whatever the explanation, "In the *History*," in the words of one scholar, "the gods are chiefly remarkable by their absence."

Thus far emphasis has been put on Thucydides as pragmatist and objective reporter, influenced by the methods and goals of medical science and by the belief that man's actions are partly determined by his innate nature and partly by the conventions of the culture into which he was born. But artistry is another equally important facet of his work. The historian fashioned a vivid, compelling narrative that draws the reader into the drama of events and engages his emotions as he experiences vicariously the pathos and suffering that war brought to the Greek world.

Nearly a century ago F.M. Cornford wrote a provocative book, *Thucydides Mythistoricus*, in which he argued that the historian's vaunted scientific objectivity was but a veneer: myth and tragedy were what had influenced his thinking, which was far closer to that of Herodotus than most were willing to admit. The narrative, he argued, is shaped to show the disastrous results of man overextending himself: as his power and riches increase, he subjects himself to the inevitable swing of fortune's pendulum in the other direction. Chance, divine displeasure and blindness to his true situation lead inexorably to disaster. Athens is the tragic heroine in the Thucydidean drama, he argues; the historian aims to rouse pity and fear in the reader on beholding the imperial city succumbing to a fatal flaw in her character and suffering a reversal of fortune.

Now there is no denying that a number of speakers in the history warn of the perils of excess and emphasize how forces outside man's control can frustrate his ambition. But that such views would be held by many participants in the war and that Thucydides would reproduce them in his history are what we would expect: we see them in the tragedians and in Herodotus, after all. But it is no guarantee that Thucydides himself believed them. Nor do I think he did. It is true that Athens suffered a great disaster: she ought to have won the war, as Pericles had said, but did not. She overextended herself, notably in the Sicilian expedition, and failed. Many accidents frustrated her plans, like the plague, Alcibiades' fall from grace after the expedition was underway and the eclipse of the moon that paralyzed the superstitious Nicias. Such features smack of tragic drama, but they have not been invented or misused to achieve their effect, but arise from the subject matter itself. Nor are they to be explained by positing a balancing scale operated by some suprahuman force at work in the world. Quite the contrary. Thucydides makes it clear that Athens' failure was the result of mistakes and misjudgments, and especially of the devastating impact the war had upon her institutions and national character.

The historian's account of the Sicilian expedition in Books 6 and 7 was admired in antiquity and has been much praised in modern times for its energy and vividness: the reader feels himself to be a spectator of the action and is swept up in the ongoing rush of events. A great seesaw of emotions animates the initial phases as the expedition is debated, voted and sent off in a scene of high hope and pageantry. Then the general Alcibiades, who had been the expedition's most vehement advocate, is suddenly recalled to stand trial on a charge of impiety, leaving his two fellow generals to carry on. The narrative concentrates now on Sicily and especially Syracuse, and is interpunctuated with Spartan moves to seize and permanently occupy the fortress at Decelea in Attic territory, at the suggestion of the by-now exiled Alcibiades. After a series of successes and some reverses in Sicily, the second general, Demosthenes, is killed. Nicias alone remains, who had initially opposed the expedition but had been chosen one of its leaders despite his misgivings. The narrative focus constricts further, fixing now on the harbor at Syracuse, as the Athenians besiegers become the besieged after a series of accidents and blunders. The claustrophobic conclusion ends in the ghastly scene in the Syracusan quarries where the remnants of what had been a huge and flourishing force meet their end. The relentless thrust of the narrative, the constricting of the focus and the pathos of the closing scenes make for intense and harrowing reading.

The overall effect is achieved with relatively little authorial comment. On the surface, the facts are made to speak for themselves, which in itself contributes to the narrative's power. Yet there is much adroitness in the seemingly absent commentator, for by selection and juxtaposition of material, by emphasis given to selected incidents and especially through graphic representation, Thucydides shapes the material to his own ends. The reader is made to see the action as if through a roving camera—a camera that has been positioned and focused by the artful historian. Irony of theme and juxtaposition contribute to the effect. The latter is strikingly illustrated by the back-to-back placement of Athens' annihilation of the insignificant island of Melos (the men who were captured were massacred, the women and children sold into slavery) with her decision to conquer all of Sicily (the last chapter of Book 5 and the first of 6). The figure of Nicias, too, is beset by many ironies. Pious, conservative, an opponent of the expedition, he is a Spartan in Athenian clothing. By a series of accidents it is he who ends up carrying out the grandiose scheme; but caution, a concern to maintain a reputation for integrity and fear of the wrath of the Athenian populace should he fail (7.48) all contribute to that failure. His death was ignominious (7.86): "Of the Greeks of my day he was the least deserving of such a fate because of his complete devotion to living a life of honor."

Thucydides makes it clear that once the expedition reached Sicily it foundered because of a series of misjudgments and mischances. But the most fundamental reason for its failure, he says early in the history (2.65), was not so much miscalculation of the island's size and power as not sending out reinforcements and supplies to bolster the troops already there. This prosaic point (which gets rather lost in the narration itself) leaves no room for positing some cosmic force that is bringing Athens low because of hubris. With proper follow-up, he is implying, even this harebrained scheme could have been pulled off successfully. The reason the Athenians failed to give adequate and continuing support to the forces in Sicily, he continues, was because their energies were concentrated on the political infighting waged by those seeking popular favor in order to enhance their personal political fortunes. These persons (here unnamed) are contrasted with Pericles, who by integrity and sheer force of personality was able to lead the people rather than being led by them: "What was ostensibly a democracy became under him rule by its leading citizen." Athens' ultimate failure in the war was due not to her defeat in Sicily, the subsequent revolt of many of her subject states or the money Sparta received from Persia to build a Peloponnesian navy: "They lost for no other reason than crippling dissensions within the city."

Here we are near the heart of Thucydides' interpretation of the conflict and its effects. The popular assembly under the pressures of war and plague was incapable of steady, foresighted governance on its own. It needed the firm hand of a statesman like Pericles. What it got after his death was a series of lesser men who pandered to the people's moods and whims in order to further their own interests (2.65); of these Cleon is the most egregious example. Democracy, in other words, proved an erratic and unreliable institution under the impact of a long and disastrous war. At 8.97 he says that rule by the Four Hundred, established in the wake of the political turmoil that followed upon the Sicilian disaster, was the best form of government at Athens in his day. It was a well-judged blend of democracy and oligarchy, he continues, which enabled Athens to start back on the road to recovery after the many reverses she had suffered. In describing the establishment of the Four Hundred he singles out two of its leaders for special praise, Antiphon the orator and Theramenes (8.68).

In all this an aristocratic, even elitist, tone is evident. Yet the historian was undoubtedly correct in pointing to the instability of the democracy as the prime factor in Athens' loss. But one wonders about his view of Pericles and of his political legacy. His remarks at 2.65 suggest that Pericles succeeded as a statesmen almost in spite of democracy, not because of it. Balancing this is the famous funeral oration (2.35–46) in which Pericles lauds the temper, ethos and institutions of Athens; he goes so far as to claim that Athenian democracy is a model for others to imitate (2.37). The nature of the occasion on which the speech was delivered helps to explain its optimism, noble and heartfelt though it is. In his last speech the bright hope of the funeral oration has dimmed and some of its claims are amended, particularly in regard to Athens' empire (compare, for example, 2.41 with 2.63); again, the change is due partly to the occasion, which comes after the outbreak of the plague and Sparta's second invasion of Attica.

In the history Pericles is more a speaker than a doer; his role in helping to create Athens' radical democracy is barely acknowledged. Criticism is made of his successors for failing to be strong leaders; yet even he had a difficult time in controlling the people, as Thucydides admits: in 430 BC their disaffection led to his suspension from office and the imposition of a heavy fine (2.59, 65). One wonders how sure his leadership would have been in some of the later crises in which the populace proved equally volatile, if not more so. More worrisome is his advice on how to win the war: namely, to attempt no new expansion, to avoid putting the city at hazard and to remain quiet (1.144, 2.65). Sensible as this is, it is at variance with the basic nature of the Athenian people, as described by the Corinthians (1.70–71) and twice endorsed by the historian himself (4.55, 8.96): restless, aggressive and always ready to enter on fresh and daring enterprises. Alcibiades, who is in many ways Pericles' successor and is in most respects an archetypal

Athenian, in arguing in favor of the Sicilian expedition, decries the do-nothing policy advocated by Nicias. Remaining quiet blunts the vigor and preparedness of a city, he says; fresh enterprises give it new experience and improve its defensive capability:

> I am convinced that a city not inactive by nature would quickly ruin itself by adopting a policy of inaction, and those are least at risk who least deviate from the character and institutions of their country, even ones that are not of the best.
>
> (6.18)

This last phrase has an ominous ring in view of what the reader knows is to come. Even before the war broke out Pericles has a foreboding of what lies ahead, much in the manner of certain characters in tragedy or wise adviser figures in Herodotus:

> I have many other reasons for expecting that we will prevail, provided you do not expand your empire in the course of the war and do not voluntarily engage in dangerous ventures. In fact, I fear your own mistakes more than I do the enemy's designs.
>
> (1.144)

Pericles is therefore a problematic figure in Thucydides. There are a number of other personalities and policies in the history that pose similar dilemmas as to what the historian thought about them or meant the reader to think. In days past many tended to explain such puzzles in terms of the Thucydidean Question: answers were predicated on the belief that the historian wrote up different sections at different times. Important as this factor might be (if it is true), there is another way of looking at the problem. This is predicated on the belief that the changing nature of the conflict brought corresponding changes in the psychology and behavior of the participants and that Thucydides means the reader to appreciate these developments as the narrative unfolds. The question is not what Thucydides thought about a topic in absolute terms but how as a historian he saw its formulation changing over time. Thus Pericles is not a monolithic figure, nor are his policies of timeless applicability. This is evident even over short stretches of time, such as the months that elapsed between the funeral oration and his last speech. It is also evident over long periods. One doubts that Pericles or anyone else expected the war to last twenty-seven years; in any case, what had seemed likely and sensible at its start became less so as the years passed, particularly as a new generation grew up: when the conflict ended people in their mid-twenties had known only war and had never known Pericles. As the narrative moves forward the attentive reader will wonder whether his advice to be quiet and take no risks was wise or possible, given the violent and erratic pressures war brought to bear on the mercurial temper of the Athenian people over so many years.

Behavior changed in the course of the war. Thucydides emphasizes two aspects in particular: the breakdown in communication and the increase in violence. As for the former, he is at pains to show how words and beliefs became twisted and lost their meaning. We see the beginning of this trend at the start, when the Corinthians criticize the Spartans for being slow to act and for their conservatism (1.70); these are not defects but virtues, King Archidamus retorts (1.84), and they are responsible for Sparta's strength and durability. Later, when the conflict is underway and the pressures of all-out war begin to be felt, rhetorical posturing becomes ever more extreme as men endeavor to cloak bad or partisan behavior under fair-sounding names. By the time we come to the revolution at Corcyra, Thucydides says (3.82), harebrained recklessness was styled courage, sensible caution was branded cowardice, steering a middle course was labeled spinelessness. And as the war progressed further, people began to say openly what they would have suppressed or palliated before: the naked imperialism expressed in the Melian Dialogue is the most striking example. "We are only acting according to the dictates of human nature," becomes the rallying cry of those justifying their acts: "You would do the same in our position."

Increase in violent behavior is a second important theme. When Mitylene revolted there was contentious debate in the Athenian assembly in which pity won out over savagery in a close vote. Ten years later we find no debate or even the pretense of one: Melos, a weak and neutral island, is wiped out because it refused to surrender on demand. Thucydides stresses the acts of unparalleled savagery as the war psychosis deepened—the frightful factional violence in Corcyra, for example, or such brutal acts as the sack of the small Boeotian town of Mycalessus by Thracian mercenaries, who killed everything that crossed their path, animal and human, including a school crowded with frightened children (7.29).

This is the grim lesson of Thucydides' history:

In peace and prosperity cities and individuals have nobler sentiments because they are not subjected to imperious necessities. But war takes away the ease of daily living and proves to be a violent teacher, putting men's impulses on the same level with their fortunes.

(3.82)

In his opening sentence Thucydides says the Peloponnesian War was the greatest upheaval the Greek world had ever known. It was suggested earlier that he felt himself in some sense to be in competition with Herodotus and Homer, and so wrote the *Archaeology* which follows to prove that his war was larger and more destructive than either the Trojan or Persian conflicts had been. But more is at issue than literary rivalry. The Peloponnesian War was horrific because of the unprecedented destruction and suffering it caused. This came about because the conflict lasted for nearly a generation and because eventually most of the Greek world was drawn into it. Most of all, it unleashed the worse impulses of man's nature, which had a long time and a wide field to display itself, as the civilized veneer of Hellenic culture cracked and fell away.

6

FOURTH-CENTURY AND HELLENISTIC HISTORIOGRAPHY

XENOPHON

In the Roman and Byzantine periods the Greeks looked back to Herodotus, Thucydides and Xenophon as the three great exemplars of classical historiography. Nowadays Xenophon has been demoted: in intellect and insight he seems to us inferior to his two predecessors. One reason the ancients admired him was his supple Attic Greek: distinguished style was highly valued and was an important factor in earning a writer a place in the school curriculum and in being held up as a model for imitation. Another reason for Xenophon's popularity was the variety of his writings, among which his philosophical ones held a high place. In fact, for much of antiquity Xenophon seems to have enjoyed greater fame as a philosopher than as a historian. He was an admirer of Socrates and had known him personally. The easy accessibility of such works as the *Memorabilia*, or Recollections of Socrates, won the author a wide readership and made him the equal of Plato in many minds as an expounder of Socratic doctrine. In antiquity and the Renaissance the most famous and influential of his works was the lengthy *Education of Cyrus*, a romanticized historical novel in which the founder of the Persian Empire is depicted as an example of what the ideal ruler should be. The ethical principles according to which Cyrus is said to have been educated are based on those that Xenophon ascribes to Socrates. A number of other works have come down to us, including a laudatory biography of the Spartan king Agesilaus and treatises on estate management, hunting, horsemanship and the duties of a cavalry commander.

Two historical works survive, the first entitled *Anabasis*, or March Up Country, the second *Hellenica*, or A History of Greece, each in seven books (although these are not the original, or Xenophon's own, divisions). The *Anabasis* describes events of 401–399 BC in which more than ten thousand Greek mercenaries joined the forces of the pretender to the Persian throne, Cyrus the Younger, in his unsuccessful attempt to depose his older brother, Artaxerxes II. At Cyrus' defeat and death at the Battle of Cunaxa (not far from Babylon), these Greeks found themselves alone in the center of the Persian Empire. The rest of the *Anabasis* describes the escape of the Ten Thousand and their reemergence in Greek lands. The *Hellenica* is a history of Greece that continues Thucydides' history where it breaks off in the year 411 and brings the narrative down to the Battle of Mantinea in 362, in which Thebes defeated Sparta but lost her great leader, Epaminondas.

Xenophon was born an Athenian in the early years of the Peloponnesian War, around 428. At the end of the war in 404 Sparta tore down the Long Walls, expelled the democrats and established an oligarchy known as the Thirty Tyrants. A reign of terror ensued in which the Thirty are said to have executed some 1,500 men for their political sympathies, their wealth or both. But a group of democratic exiles managed to recapture Athens' port city of Piraeus and to defeat the troops of the Thirty. By June 403 full democracy was reestablished, with Spartan acquiescence. Xenophon seems to have been a supporter of the Thirty, at least in the early stages of their regime, and presents a sympathetic portrait of Theramenes, the head of the more moderate faction among the ruling oligarchs. Theramenes was put to death by the radical element led by Critias, who was a second cousin of Plato and who, like Xenophon, had been an associate of Socrates. In any event, the young Xenophon seems to have had few prospects for advancement in Athens after the fall of the Thirty. He therefore accepted the proposal of his friend Proxenus of Boeotia to join the expedition of the younger Cyrus, a supporter of Sparta in the closing years of the Peloponnesian War. When Xenophon asked Socrates about the wisdom of his going (*Anabasis* 3.1.4–10), he was advised to consult Apollo at Delphi. In a question reminiscent of the one Croesus once posed, he asked Apollo to what gods he should sacrifice in order to make the journey; on his return from Delphi, Socrates rebuked him for not asking whether it would be wise for him to go in the first place, "but since he did not so ask, he ought, he said, to do what the god commanded."

Xenophon had no official position in the expedition, but went because Proxenus promised to make him friends with Cyrus (*Anabasis* 3.1.4). Moreover, the announced goal of Cyrus was to conduct a local punitive raid against the Pisidians, who inhabited an area in what is now southwestern Turkey. But Cyrus led them far beyond Pisidia; only later, when it was too late to turn back, did they learn his real aim was to overthrow his brother. Xenophon shows no animus against Cyrus for this deception; in fact, he praises him greatly as man and commander (1.9.28): "Based on what I have heard, I believe no one has ever been beloved by more people, Greeks or barbarians."

After their escape, the Ten Thousand gradually broke up. In the next years Xenophon took service in a number of campaigns in the Aegean area, including some under Spartan commanders, particularly King Agesilaus. Sometime during this period he was banished from Athens, possibly for joining the expedition of Cyrus, who had been an enemy of Athens, and certainly for his devotion to Spartan interests. Xenophon went into exile in the Peloponnesus and was given an estate near Olympia by the Spartans. There he lived as a country gentleman until the fateful Battle of Leuctra in 371 when Thebes defeated Sparta, in consequence of which he lost his estate and migrated to Corinth. Shortly thereafter, when Athens concluded an alliance with Sparta, Xenophon's decree of banishment was lifted. He sent his two sons to serve in the Athenian cavalry, although it was at Corinth that he is said to have died, in the later 350s.

The *Anabasis* is a taut and exciting memoir, narrated in the third person. It is studded with speeches, including some by Xenophon himself. It might better have been entitled *Katabasis*, or March Down Country, since the bulk of the story concerns the adventures of the Ten Thousand after Cunaxa. When their leaders were treacherously murdered by the Persian satrap Tissaphernes, Xenophon took over as one of the two chief commanders in the Ten Thousand's harrowing escape in midwinter through the snowy mountains of Kurdistan and Armenia. A particularly memorable moment comes when the Black Sea is first sighted, which for a Greek meant they were nearing Hellenic lands. When the shouting began in the front line, Xenophon and his men in the rear feared that the enemy was attacking. But as the word was passed down, everyone surged forward shouting "The sea! The sea!" A scene of tearful euphoria ensues, as the men gaze down from the heights on the sparkling waters (*Anabasis* 4.7.21–27).

Although Xenophon composed the *Anabasis* many years after the event, it retains great vigor and freshness. Some have supposed that what prompted him to write were other accounts of the Ten Thousand that Xenophon felt were wrong or unfair to himself. The evidence for this is speculative, although it might be so. A more powerful reason is the fame that the expedition had acquired over the years, and particularly the weakness of the Persian Empire that the escape of the Ten Thousand seemed to have revealed. There were calls, particularly on the part of the famous rhetorician Isocrates (e.g. *Panegyricus* 173–174, 380 BC), for the Greeks to rid themselves of their internecine conflicts by uniting against Persia in a panhellenic effort to bring down the Great King. It was in this climate of opinion that Xenophon composed his *Anabasis*. He himself heartily subscribed to the idea of panhellenism and at the start of the *Anabasis* points out how vulnerable Persia was to attack (1.5.9). The work doubtless added to the idea's momentum, which Isocrates continued to champion and which Alexander the Great was destined to realize some decades later.

The *Hellenica*, by contrast, is uneven and sometimes disappointing. It may have been written in two stages some years apart. The first (to 2.3.10) continues Thucydides' history from 411 to the end of the war in 404 and uses the earlier historian's dating by summers and winters. The first words comprise one of the oddest openings in literature: ‚"After these events, Thymochares came from Athens not many days later with a few ships." That this is a continuation is obvious; the join, however, is not exact. When Thucydides' text breaks off the scene is at Ephesus, whereas Xenophon begins with events in the Hellespont. Although wishing to continue Thucydides, he evidently did not want to begin in mid episode; a slight forward jump in chronology results, as the words "not many days later" indicate. The narrative of the remaining years of the war is brisk and selective. Clearly Xenophon's aim was simply to complete an account of the war, not to imitate or rival Thucydides. The second stage, which was finished after the Battle of Mantinea in 362 BC, abandons dating by summers and winters and becomes a general history of Greece over the next forty-two years. This part opens with an lively and detailed account of the Thirty, featuring full-length speeches, high drama and well-drawn portraits (2.3.11–2.4.43). But thereafter the work becomes erratic and something of a patchwork, with glaring omissions (for example, he says not a word about the establishment of the Second Athenian Confederacy in the 370s BC) and with distortions owing to a bias in favor of Sparta (her role in establishing the Thirty is wholly suppressed, for example) and against the power that twice defeated her in this period, Thebes. In fact, Xenophon in his account of the Battle of Leuctra in 371 does not even mention Thebes' great commander, Epaminondas, although he does name him late in the work (7.1.41) and near the end gives a handsome if belated tribute to his military expertise (7.5.6–9). It should be added that

Xenophon is not consistently partisan; he can be quite critical of Sparta at times.

The *Hellenica* concludes with a frank admission: the struggle of the Greek city states to win supremacy over one another has resulted in no clear winner; history seems to be going nowhere, although the author hopes his work will find a continuator (the phrase "after these events" echoes the opening words):

> Following the battle, confusion and turmoil became even greater throughout Greece than before. I am going to conclude my narrative at this point. Perhaps someone else will concern himself with what happened after these events.
>
> (7.5.27)

So ends the *Hellenica*.

Xenophon describes events that he witnessed himself, such as those concerning the Thirty and the Ten Thousand, in a lively, sometimes penetrating, manner. Few writers of his age were so well positioned to write contemporary history as he was, given his military experience, his knowledge of distant places and his acquaintance with many of the leading figures of the time. But when he relies on the reports of others, his grasp of the scope, interrelation and significance of events weakens. At times he seems to be writing the history of Greece as if it were a memoir, basing it on whatever news chanced to reach him in whatever place he chanced to be; he does not seem to have spent much time or effort in cross-checking these reports or in securing information from a wider spectrum of sources (5.4.7 is the only notice of an alternate account in the *Hellenica*).

Admittedly the history of Greece from 404 to 362 BC is a confusing period. The seesaw battle for domination waged by Sparta, Athens and Thebes produced no clear winner, while the calculated infusion of Persian money from time to time contributed to the instability. So in some respects one can sympathize with Xenophon's unhappiness in the aftermath of Mantinea. But it is difficult to see what prompted him in the first place to write of a period he found difficult to make sense of. He was certainly among the first to write such a comprehensive history of contemporary Greece, and probably was the very first. If he was trying to correct or improve on someone else's general history, there is no evidence for it in his text and not even an obvious candidate given our present knowledge, save possibly for the Oxyrhynchus historian (see below).

Particularly striking is the fact that Xenophon mentions scarcely any other historian, living or dead, and has no seeming quarrel with any other writer. In this regard he stands virtually alone among the Greek historians, a contentious crew who relished attacking one another for mendacity and incompetence. There is none of this in Xenophon. Moreover, both the *Anabasis* and the *Hellenica* lack a preface announcing the author's name and subject, which was the standard way of of beginning a history before and after Xenophon. Equally surprising, in the *Hellenica* (3.1.2) he refers to the *Anabasis* as the work of one Themistogenes of Syracuse, which has deceived scarcely anyone now or in antiquity (cf. Plutarch, *Moralia* 345E), and to himself simply as "the commander of the troops that had served with Cyrus" (3.2.7). Personal reticence is also shown in his description of an Athenian cavalry engagement at Mantinea prior to the main battle (*Hellenica* 7.5.15–17). His son Gryllus perished in the fight, dying in such heroic fashion that he was later commemorated in a famous painting in the Athenian agora and by writers such as Isocrates and Aristotle. But Xenophon merely says of the fallen, "Good men among them perished." In the *Anabasis* he generally presents himself and his conduct in a favorable light; but all in all, Xenophon was a singularly self-effacing historian.

He was also a firm believer in the power of the gods to influence individual destinies and the course of history. In this, again, he stands in contrast to most other historians, even Herodotus. It is true that he invokes the gods to explain improbable outcomes (e.g. *Hellenica* 4.4.12), as Herodotus occasionally did. But he also sees the divine operating on a regular basis in daily life, including his own. Many instances could be cited. For example, Zeus sent him a dream after the Battle of Cunaxa (*Anabasis* 3.1.11–13); the entrails of sacrificial victims portended an attempt to assassinate King Agesilaus (*Hellenica* 3.3.4); when the Spartans broke their oath to the gods to let the cities of Greece be free by seizing the acropolis of Thebes, they "were punished by the very people whom they had wronged—and by them alone" (*Hellenica* 5.4.1). Tissaphernes, the Persian satrap who had murdered the Greek leaders after Cunaxa despite his oath to observe a truce, is twice said to have incurred the anger of the gods, once by King Agesilaus (*Hellenica* 3.4.11) and once by the historian himself (*Anabasis* 3.2.10).

Xenophon makes no programmatic statements on what he conceived the nature and value of history to be. But from a few asides we can see that one of his aims, like that of Herodotus, was simple commemoration. For example, in describing the loyalty to Sparta of the small Peloponnesian town of Phlius when under attack by Sparta's enemies, he says (*Hellenica* 7.2.1), "All writers mention the great deeds of large cities; but when a small one performs numerous great actions, these, I think, are even more worthy of record." What calls forth Xenophon's special commendation are the moral qualities of the Phliasians: their power to endure hardships, nobility of spirit and brave hearts. Similar qualities receive praise throughout his works, and show the influence of Socrates' ethical teachings as Xenophon understood them. Rarely he goes beyond commemoration and presents history as a repository of moral lessons that will enlighten his readers in their personal lives. The Spartan commander Teleutias is twice cited in this connection. His conduct in one campaign won such loyalty from his men that Xenophon invites his readers to consider this more impressive than the large amounts of money or the great dangers involved (*Hellenica* 5.1.4); later, when Teleutias allows his anger to get the better of his judgment in attacking another enemy and dies as a consequence, he says such examples show that anger is wrong even when punishing slaves, to say nothing of letting it get the upper hand when commanding troops (5.3.7). In Xenophon's historical narrative individuals often loom larger than groups or states, both as paradigms of conduct and as causative agents affecting the course of events.

Xenophon is often viewed as a typical upperclass Greek of his day: a keen sportsman and admirer of military discipline; conservative, devoted to traditional religion, reasonably intelligent, but not a deep thinker. But for all his conventionality in some respects, he was quite unconventional in others. A gifted stylist and literary innovator, he created new literary genres, including most probably a general history of Greece, and was able to recreate graphically the drama and personalities he had known many years before. He stood aloof from the quarrels and acrimony of his fellow philosophers and historians, writing as he thought and felt, unconcerned to place himself in the limelight. For all his failings, and despite some seemingly conventional traits, there is more to Xenophon than meets the eye and much that defies easy categorization.

FRAGMENTARY HISTORIANS

A canon of ten leading Greek historians from late antiquity includes the following: Herodotus, Thucydides, Xenophon, Philistus, Theopompus, Ephorus, Anaximenes, Callisthenes, Hellanicus and

Polybius (*FGrH* 70 T34). The first three and the last survive; the rest do not. It is no accident that none of them wrote in the period after the death of Alexander the Great in 323 BC except Polybius. In fact, *no* historian in these nearly two hundred years survives: all are represented either by fragments from their works, whether in quotation and paraphrase, or through *testimonia*: that is, comments about their lives and writings. The fragments and *testimonia* relating to lost Greek historians are contained in Felix Jacoby's *Die Fragmente der griechischen Historiker*; 856 names are included, a grim illustration of how few writers survived the wreck of antiquity (yet Jacoby lived to complete only three-quarters of his announced plan). Despite the fact that we have many fragments from some of these lost historians and hence know quite a bit about them, it is a delicate task to evaluate this information properly. Some of it has been distorted by the prejudices of others who quote or criticize them; this is true of Polybius, for example, as we will see. Other sources have special, even quirky, interests. One of these is Athenaeus, who flourished around AD 200, and who is fond of giving lengthy extracts (often quite faithful) from historians on, among other subjects, luxury and licentious living. Such sources can give a quite skewed picture of a writer unless caution and perspective are brought to bear.

One reason for the survival of Herodotus, Thucydides and Xenophon was a classicizing movement that appeared in the first century BC and continued strongly thereafter in the Greek-speaking world. By this time the Greeks had become part of the Roman Empire. In partial compensation for their loss of political independence, many looked back to the glory days of Hellas, that is, to the archaic period and to the fifth and early fourth centuries, as a source of pride and for a sense of cultural superiority. Thus, in the pantheon of great authors that formed the core of later Greek education and culture, the first three historians became the exemplars of their genre, while many historians who followed them fell into comparative neglect. Herodotus and Thucydides were especially honored. For example, Dionysius of Halicarnassus, a literary critic of the first century BC, himself a historian, wrote a separate treatise *On Thucydides*, and, when he wished to illustrate those qualities "we look for in all histories," used Herodotus and Thucydides to do so (*Letter to Pompeius* 3; see below). Their primacy continued for centuries. When Lucian in the second century AD wrote his *How to Write History*, the would-be historians he satirizes imitate Herodotus and Thucydides almost exclusively in their accounts of the Parthian War of the Roman Emperor Lucius

Verus. Four centuries later the preface to Procopius' *Persian Wars* proves to be a heady mix of Herodotean and Thucydidean reminiscences. A thousand years separates Procopius from his models.

A few years after the Battle of Mantinea in 362 BC, which Xenophon had deplored as producing no clear winner among the competing city states of Greece, a new power arose in the north in the person of Philip II, king of Macedon. He quickly showed that the solution lay with him and with his son and successor, Alexander the Great. By the time of Philip's assassination in 336 he was the dominant force in Greece. On Alexander's succession, but before departing in 334 to destroy the power of Persia, he punished the rebellious city of Thebes by razing it to the ground, sparing only the temples and the house of the poet Pindar, as an object lesson for any state that might contemplate defection during his absence. Alexander's conquest of the Persian Empire caused the whole of the East to fall into his hands, including Egypt and territories as far away as Bactria (modern Afghanistan). By the time of his premature death in 323, the horizons of the Greek-speaking world had expanded enormously; the numerous city states of old Greece found they were small players in a vast new world. What we now call the Hellenistic age had begun (323–146 BC).

The first fifty years were dominated by a struggle among Alexander's successors to keep the empire together and subject to the control of one of them. But when these conflicts ended in a stalemate, several large kingdoms emerged ruled by hereditary monarchs. Their subjects for the most part were the non-Greek natives; their regimes were maintained by Greek mercenaries and bolstered by Greek traders and immigrants. The chief dynasties were the Antigonids in Macedon, the Seleucids in Asia and parts of Asia Minor and the Ptolemies in Egypt. Certain smaller states also managed to exert influence, such as the kingdom of Pergamum in western Asia Minor and the island of Rhodes in the Aegean. States like Sparta and Athens found themselves drawn into the orbit of Macedon, which dominated most of old Greece. A loss of political importance and even at times of independence was the result. Certain city states responded by forming leagues in order to exercise greater leverage in this new world of giants. The most notable of these were the Achaean League in the Peloponnesus and the Aetolian League in northwest Greece.

The changed conditions inevitably affected the writing of history. The complex relations of far-flung empires now became the chief subject of historical writing. Histories of a size commensurate with their subjects appeared: many ran to thirty volumes and more, which, given the expense and time it took to make copies, may partly account for their failure to survive. Another effect was on the truthfulness of history: autocrats often called forth flattering portraits by those seeking to win their good will or negative portrayals by those who disliked or feared them. The audience for whom historians wrote expanded and changed also. Readers expected to be entertained as well as instructed. In the hands of some practitioners history became a substitute for the adventure novel, for others a repository of marvels and of tales involving aberrant or affecting behavior. Interest in individuals became ever more prominent, as one would expect in this world of powerful monarchs. But readers also liked at times to hear of less grand subjects, particularly human interest stories that ranged from the bizarre to the amorous.

A number of later Greek historians survive who wrote about the Roman world (Arrian's subject, however, was Alexander the Great). These include writers such as Polybius, Dionysius of Halicarnassus, Diodorus Siculus, Appian, Dio Cassius and Josephus. Even so, the works of most of these historians are not fully extant (possibly due to their length); some parts are intact, while others are represented by extracts and epitomes. One reason why these writers survived was the very fact that they wrote about the Romans. In late antiquity the Roman Empire split into two parts, one in the East, the other in the West. Constantinople, founded by Constantine the Great in AD 330, was the capital of the East, and styled itself the Second Rome. This was the beginning of the long-lived Byzantine Empire, whose language and culture were Greek, but whose political inheritance was Roman. In fact, the Byzantines called themselves *hoi Rhômaioi*, the Romans, and continued to do so up to the day in 1453 when Constantinople fell to the Turks. The fact that the Hellenistic age had the misfortune to fall between classical Greece and the Roman period is one reason for the loss of so much of its literature.

The canon of ten Greek historians cited earlier was clearly a product of the classicizing movement. All of them flourished before the death of Alexander except for Polybius. Anaximenes of Lampsacus is a somewhat surprising choice. His histories were largely eclipsed by those of others to be discussed shortly, his *Hellenica* by Ephorus, his *Philippica* by Theopompus and his history of Alexander by Callisthenes. Philistus, however, was much admired: Cicero described him as "a capital writer, pithy, penetrating, concise—almost a Thucydides in miniature" (*Letter to his Brother Quintus* 2.11); he receives praise from Dionysius as well, although he is criticized for his graceless style (*Letter to Pompeius* 7). Philistus wrote a history of Sicily from its earliest days and served in high positions under Dionysius I and II, tyrants of Syracuse, from 405 BC to his death in 356. He portrayed these two autocrats in a flattering light, although he was exiled by the former after a quarrel and recalled by the latter.

Ephorus, said to have been a pupil of the rhetorician Isocrates, as was Theopompus, wrote the first "universal" history of Greece in thirty books, starting in early times and continuing to 341 BC (his son authored the last book, presumably after his father's death). The idea of panhellenism is clearly evident in this synoptic vision of Greek history: Hellenism acquired its identity not from political unity but from a common culture and common aspirations. Each book had its own preface, and the arrangement was *kata genos* (*FGrH* 70 T11), which probably means by geographical area. Ephorus refused to go further back in time than the return to Greece of the sons of Heracles (which answers in historical terms to the arrival of the Dorian Greeks in the Peloponnesus in the eleventh century BC), declaring that myth and the distant past are unlikely to have been remembered accurately, while detailed contemporary history is the most trustworthy (*FGrH* 70 F9). He stressed the value of historical accounts based on first-hand experience (*FGrH* 70 F110), although he did not hesitate to give a circumstantial account of the doings of these sons of Heracles, as some of the fragments show (e.g. *FGrH* 70 F115). His work was never superseded; in the first century BC Diodorus Siculus used him as his chief source for Books 11–15 of his *Historical Library*, a careless compilation in which some twenty books of Ephorus have been condensed into five.

Theopompus of Chios was a prolific and opinionated writer of at least two major histories. One, called the *Hellenica*, was a continuation of Thucydides in twelve books, bringing the story down to 394 BC; its theme was the supremacy of Sparta as she first defeated Athens and then battled unsuccessfully to maintain that supremacy. It may have been meant as a riposte to Xenophon's *Hellenica* (cf. *FGrH* 115 F21). Of Theopompus' personal life, we hear that he and his father were banished from Chios for their Spartan sympathies but were later restored by order of Alexander. Theopompus clearly sympathized with oligarchies and had some trenchant criticisms to make of Athens and Athenian democracy. His second and more famous history was the *Philippica* in fifty-eight books, a vast work whose main subject was the reign of Philip II of Macedon (359–336 BC). When 150 years later

Philip V wanted those parts abstracted that pertained to his predecessor, there was material for only sixteen books; the remainder consisted of digressions, historical flashbacks and contemporary events in which Philip was not directly involved (*FGrH* 115 T31; cf. T30). Certain sections sometimes carried their own names, such as "Marvels" in parts of Books 8 and 9, or "On the Demagogues" in Book 10. We hear also of a two-volume "epitome" of Herodotus, which may have been part of the *Philippica* although cited by separate title.

Callisthenes was probably the most famous of the historians of Alexander. As a kinsman of Aristotle, Alexander's tutor, and the author of a ten-volume work covering the history of Greece from 387 to 357 BC, he was chosen to accompany the expedition to Persia as its official historian. He presented Alexander in a most flattering light, describing such miraculous incidents as how the waves of the sea withdrew and prostrated themselves as Alexander passed (*FGrH* 124 F31), or how crows guided the king and his entourage through the Egyptian desert as he sought to reach the oracular temple of Zeus Amon, where he was pronounced the son of Zeus (*FGrH* 124 F14). Although Callisthenes was willing to write of nature's obeisance to Alexander, he balked when he was required to prostrate himself before the king in oriental fashion, as Alexander wanted. A breach occurred; shortly thereafter Callisthenes was charged with being part of a conspiracy and was executed (324 BC).

Any modern canon of Greek historians would undoubtedly include Timaeus of Tauromenium, a Sicilian whose long life spanned the later fourth century BC and the first half of the third. After being exiled by Agathocles, tyrant of Syracuse, he went to Athens, where he spent the next fifty years doing historical research. He turned his back on Alexander and the successor states in the East, concentrating instead on a history of the West in thirty-eight books, bringing the narrative down to the crossing of the Romans into Sicily in 264 BC (*FGrH* 566 T6a). In it he included information about Carthage, Rome and events in the Greek East. He was the first to introduce into history dating by Olympiads, four-year periods beginning with the first Olympiad in 776 BC. Polybius, as we will see, attacked him trenchantly and at length on many grounds. Yet, however justified some of this criticism may have been, Polybius clearly felt Timaeus to be a major rival who enjoyed an enviable reputation. He himself credits Timaeus with having accurately established Olympiad dating, some of it based on inscriptional evidence, and adopts it for his own history (12.11.1–3). Timaeus was a sharp critic of other writers. He implied that Plato was guilty of plagiarism and called Aristotle "a pedantic and detestable sophist" (*FGrH* 566 FF14, 156); among historians, he is known to have attacked Thucydides, Philistus, Ephorus, Theopompus and Callisthenes.

THE VARIETIES OF HISTORY

Jacoby divided Greek historical writing into seven categories: genealogy (including mythography), ethnography, contemporary narrative history, chronography, horography or local histories, biography (including literary history) and geography. Naturally an author might write a number of works of different types or combine many in a single work, as Theopompus did in his *Philippica*. Within narrative history, which is the focus of the present volume, various permutations appeared, most early on in the development of historical writing.

Local histories began in the latter half of the fifth century. They tended to concentrate on the myths and legends of a city, particularly in connection with its founding, including topics like religious customs and genealogies. The city's history would be sketched out in a year-by-year format, and brought down to the lifetime of the author. Especially notable were those who wrote on Athens and Attica, the so-called Atthidographers (the individual work being called an *Atthis*, pl. *Atthides*). Hellanicus of Lesbos toward the end of the fifth century BC, one of the ten canonical historians, was reckoned the first author of an Athenian history (he also wrote on other cities and countries, and on myths and chronology). Thucydides criticizes him by name at 1.97 for sketchy and inaccurate chronology in the period between the Persian and Peloponnesian Wars: that is, for events of Hellanicus' own lifetime (Thucydides' own chronology for this period is not above reproach, however). Later well-known Atthidographers were Androtion in the fourth century BC and Philochorus in the third. Other cities had their local historians. For example, Ephorus wrote of his native town, Cyme, while both he and Theopompus of Chios referred to their places of birth frequently—sometimes unnecessarily—in their historical works. A special branch of local history focused on the political constitutions of states. The best known of these were the 158 Greek constitutions (including a few non-Greek) that were compiled by Aristotle or under his direction in the fourth century as materials for the study of political philosophy. His *Constitution of Athens* was found in papyrus form at the end of the nineteenth century.

111

Related to local histories were regional histories, both Greek and non-Greek. We have seen that Philistus wrote of Sicily and Timaeus of the West generally, although his major emphasis was also on Sicily. Others featured such exotic places as India (e.g. Megasthenes), Egypt (e.g. Hecataeus of Abdera) or the Red Sea (Agatharchides). Persia continued to stimulate curiosity. Ctesias of Cnidus was personal physician to Artaxerxes II and was present at the Battle of Cunaxa in 401 BC in which Cyrus the Younger lost his life and which Xenophon chronicled in his *Anabasis*. In his writing Ctesias criticized and contradicted many points in Herodotus about Persia and India. Yet he himself sometimes reported even more improbable marvels than had his predecessor. For example, he told of cattle belonging to the Great King that knew how to count to a hundred (*FGrH* 688 F34). He also described the frightful martichora (Persian for "man-eater"— a tiger?), with a human face and double rows of teeth, which shot death-dealing darts out of its tail, a specimen of which Ctesias affirms he saw with his own eyes (*FGrH* 688 F45d). In reaction to Greek tales of foreign places, Hellenized barbarians wrote of their native lands in the Greek language: Berossus on Babylon and Manetho on Egypt (Manetho's list of kings and dynasties still form the basis of ancient Egyptian chronology).

Herodotus had many followers in the centuries after his death. Dionysius argues that Xenophon modeled himself on Herodotus in both subject matter and language, despite his being a continuator of Thucydides (*Letter to Pompeius* 4). Interest in the geography and ethnography of foreign lands, especially Persia, Egypt and India, continued strongly, and was obviously given a further boost by the conquests of Alexander. Yet it was the fashion to criticize Herodotus as a teller of tall tales, as the mendacious Ctesias did. Such criticisms were meant to assert an author's superiority and independence; at the same time they testify to how widely Herodotus was read in this period. Theopompus' numerous and extensive digressions in his *Philippica* are clearly in the Herodotean tradition, to say nothing of his "epitome" of that author, while Callisthenes was said to have followed Herodotus closely in some of his descriptions (*FGrH* 124 F38).

Thucydides had at least three continuators, possibly four:- Xenophon and Theopompus, already mentioned, and Cratippus and the Oxyrhynchus historian. Little is known of Cratippus except that he admired Thucydides, employed no speeches (in this following Thucydides in his eighth book) and wrote of the period from 411 to the late 390s BC (*FGrH* 64 T2, F1), the same period that Theopompus covered in his *Hellenica*. The Oxyrhynchus historian is represented in an extensive passage preserved on papyrus, which gives a detailed account of the years 396–395 BC. Its dry factual precision, together with dating by summers and winters, show that this was an attempt not only to continue Thucydides, but to imitate him in technique and format. Much effort has been made to put a name to its author. Theopompus was once touted, but few now think this to be right. The quality of this fragment makes it likely, as one scholar has said, that the author is someone we know rather than someone we do not. Nowadays a number of advocates for Cratippus have appeared, which seems the most economical solution. Thucydides had other admirers and imitators. Philistus, already mentioned, was one: "a Thucydides in miniature." In fact, in his description of the Athenian defeat at Syracuse Philistus followed Thucydides' account very closely despite the fact that he himself had been an eyewitness, whereas Thucydides had not (*FGrH* 556 F51). Another author who seems much in the Thucydidean tradition was Hieronymus of Cardia, whose history of Alexander's successors carried down to the 270s BC: an experienced soldier and active diplomat, and an exile from his native city, he wrote a sober and serious account of events in which he had participated and about persons he had known. His work forms the basis of Books 18–20 of Diodorus' *Historical Library*.

RHETORICAL HISTORY

In the fourth century BC the practice and theory of rhetoric came into their own, the spoken word exemplified in such orators as Demosthenes, the written word in teachers like Isocrates, while Aristotle and others developed the theoretical underpinnings of the subject. Rhetoric had an immediate effect on the writing of history. Philistus, who died in 356, was "the first to write history in accordance with the rules of rhetoric" (*FGrH* 556 T1); of his immediate successors Ephorus wrote a treatise on style, while Theopompus was almost as famous as an epideictic orator as an historian.

Speeches in historical works began to be composed according to rhetorical precepts that governed the argumentation and arrangement of material. And since rhetoric was also concerned with language and style, it affected the narrative as well: prose rhythm, vocabulary, figures of thought and speech, the shape of sentences and the like. Rhetoric also operated on a less obvious level, since it was at bottom concerned with successful techniques of reasoning and persuasion.

Students were taught how to discover the most suitable arguments for a particular situation and audience, such as those deriving from utility, honor and probability. Arguments from honor were based on ethics and morality: what was just, religiously right, civilized, meritorious and so forth. Arguments from probability were based on personality types: what an individual was likely to do, given his character and situation, or how a particular audience was likely to respond, given its nature and prejudices. The aim of rhetoric was to subjugate the reader to the writer's will, Isocrates declared. It was therefore as much concerned with pleasure as with instruction, since pleasure was the vehicle that would make the audience receptive to instruction.

Aristotle distinguished three types of oratory: forensic, deliberative and epideictic. The first applied to the courtroom, where the truth of a past event was in question, the second to groups debating the best course to take for the future. The third, "display" oratory, featured speeches of praise or blame, usually delivered on ceremonial occasions. Most speeches in histories were of the deliberative type, although occasionally forensic and epideictic speeches would find a place (Pericles' funeral speech in Thucydides is epideictic).

In the hands of some practitioners speeches now took on an even greater role than they had before: there were more of them and the argumentation might derive less from the realities of the historical situation than from the precepts of the rhetorical handbooks. Polybius criticizes Timaeus for just these failings and cites several of his speeches as examples (12.25i–26b). One of these was delivered by Hermocrates of Syracuse in 424 BC to delegates from Sicilian cities who were aiming to thwart Athens' attempt to build up a coalition of states favorable to her. We have Thucydides' version of this speech at 4.59–64 (although Polybius does not refer to it). The Thucydidean Hermocrates begins by saying it would be pointless to catalog the evils of war (4.59). The Timaean Hermocrates, after complimenting his audience for being men who know the difference between the blessings of peace and the evils of war, proceeds to give a series of commonplaces illustrative of just this point ("sleepers awake to the cockcrow in peace, to the bugle in war" and so forth); he then adds some extended quotations from Homer and Euripides by way of corroboration before reverting to more commonplaces ("war is like sickness and peace is like health," etc.). All this, growls Polybius, is the sort of stuff a schoolboy would produce for a homework assignment, not what an experienced statesman like Hermocrates would have said.

During the third century a new style developed under the impetus of rhetoric, called Asian because it first appeared and flourished in the Greek cities of Asia Minor. It tended to the sententious and ornamental, with much attention paid to rhythm and poeticisms (Timaeus wrote in this fashion). In its more extreme form Asianism became florid and emotional, stressing agitated rhythms, bold metaphors and lush verbal effects. We have a fragment in this mode from the historian Hegesias of Magnesia, who wrote a history of Alexander:

> In destroying Thebes, Alexander, you did what Zeus would do were he to cast down the moon from its place in the sky above (for the sun I reserve as the symbol of Athens). These two cities were the eyesight of Hellas. Therefore I now bemoan the fate of one of them, for one eye, the Theban town, has been knocked out.
>
> (FGrH 142 F12)

No effort has been made here to reproduce the rhythms, poeticisms and unusual word order. But what remains is enough to illustrate the style. The forced and frigid mixing of metaphors, the direct address to Alexander and the author's avowal of his personal distress seem more suited, as one scholar has said, to the chorus of a third-rate tragedy than to historical exposition. This passage is doubtless extreme, and probably does not represent Asianism in its everyday guise. The style prevailed for two centuries before a reaction set in, when, under the aegis of the classicizing movement, the Attic prose of earlier days came into vogue.

ETHICAL HISTORY

Recording praiseworthy behavior was intrinsic to history from the start. In his opening sentence Herodotus says that he writes "so that man's past may not fade into oblivion over time nor the great and amazing deeds displayed by both Greeks and barbarians be without renown." Occasionally he will highlight bad conduct, such as that of the traitor Ephialtes (7.214): "I put his name on record as the guilty one." This commemorative function of history continued in the fourth century and Hellenistic age. Callisthenes undiplomatically declared that fame would come to Alexander through his histories, not to himself through association with Alexander (FGrH 124 T8).

To this commemorative aim were added others of an ethical nature. One was the growing conviction that to his account of what people did

115

the historian should append his personal judgments about the goodness and badness of their behavior (obituary notices became a favored place to put them). It was not enough to let the narrative speak for itself; the historian was to step forward in his own person. Nor was this an option the historian might choose; by the time of Polybius it was considered an absolute duty (1.14, 8.10, 10.21, 12.15, 16.28). Rhetoric was a strong influence here, since the subject matter of epideictic oratory was precisely praise and blame. Philistus included passages of praise and blame, we hear (*FGrH* 556 T16b), and we have seen Xenophon sometimes pointing out to the reader the praiseworthy nature of certain states and individuals. Perhaps the one who used this technique to its most striking effect was Theopompus, who, we are told (*FGrH* 115 T20), had the uncanny ability to ferret out all the varieties of seeming virtue and undetected vice, and was compared in severity to the fabled judges of the Underworld interrogating the dead souls who came before their tribunal. Theopompus was particularly harsh on the misbehavior of Philip II of Macedon, castigating his drunkenness, womanizing and faithlessness (*FGrH* 115 FF27, 225).

During the Hellenistic age this ethical approach was widened to include a new purpose: history can benefit the reader by featuring paradigms of conduct that he may imitate or avoid in his personal life. History, in other words, can lead to moral improvement; it was on its way to becoming "philosophy teaching by examples," which was a popular definition in the Roman period. We get a hint of this in Xenophon when he tells the reader that the example of Teleutias shows anger to be as destructive in private life as in the public sphere (*Hellenica* 5.3.7). By the time of Polybius this purpose is fully acknowledged (1.1, 10.21). A further effect is the belief that history will act as a stimulus to people to behave honorably, knowing that their conduct will be written up for everyone to read. Conversely, in several prefaces of Diodorus (which are probably based on earlier sources, particularly Ephorus), we hear that evildoers will be deterred from behaving badly when they realize history will find them out and blazon their misconduct on its pages for all posterity to know (1.1, 14.1, 15.1).

BIOGRAPHICAL HISTORY

The prominence of individuals in the works of Xenophon and Philistus quickly led to histories that focused on a single person. The first example was Theopompus' *Philippica* in fifty-eight books:

"The Age of Philip." Polybius' reaction was this: "It would have been finer and more fitting to include the deeds of Philip in the history of Greece than the history of Greece in that of Philip" (8.11). But Theopompus' choice of subject was justified, since Philip's genius and initiative transformed Macedon from a backward state to the dominant power in Greece in less than twenty-five years: it was around him that the history of mainland Greece was centered in this period. On the other hand, Theopompus depicted Philip and his associates in the blackest colors—as drunkards, degenerates and liars; Polybius makes the reasonable objection that Theopompus' dismissive picture fails to explain how such men could have had the talent and energy to subdue Greece, overthrow the Persian Empire and establish the successor states (8.9–10). Of course, the career of his son Alexander gave rise to a veritable mini-industry in biographical history. Over twenty writers are known to have made Alexander their subject, among them Callisthenes, Nearchus, Aristobulus and Ptolemy.

It is clear that at bottom biographical history was a type of ethical history. The requirement that a historian judge the goodness and badness of the individuals in his narrative made a strong ethical slant inevitable. Such appraisals, however, laid the writer open to criticism. If he gave a negative portrait, as Theopompus did of Philip or Timaeus did of Agathocles, one could say with Polybius that the bias of the historian blinded him to the good points in an otherwise bad character (8.10–11, 12.15). On the other hand, if a writer praised a great man whom he had known and had served under, one could lable him a toady of a powerful benefactor. Philistus was pilloried for his favorable portraits of the two Dionysii (*FGrH* 556 T13), while Callisthenes, Timaeus affirmed, deserved the execution he suffered at Alexander's hands, whose mind he had corrupted by gross flattery (*FGrH* 124 T20).

This type of history should not be confused with biography per se, which throughout antiquity was regarded as a separate genre. Biography aimed to reveal a man's character by describing his childhood and through telling anecdotes, which might be embedded in incidents of a quite trifling sort, rather than in great battles or other momentous events (see Plutarch, *Alexander* 1); occasionally historians would also include such anecdotes, but often with an apology (e.g. Xenophon, *Hellenica* 2.3.53). Moreover, certain biographies might be frankly laudatory in nature, magnifying a man's achievements and highlighting him from flattering angles. So Xenophon's account of Agesilaus in the *Hellenica* is more sober and even-handed than the rosy portrait in his biography of the king (despite many close correspondences between the two works). Polybius distinguishes clearly between the way he described Philopoemen in his eulogistic biography and how he will depict him in his histories (10.21). Sometimes a biography might be cast in the form of of an outright encomium, prompting the writer to ignore the facts of history altogether. In Isocrates' life of King Evagoras of Cyprus the protagonist is not assassinated in an unseemly palace intrigue, as he was in real life, but is simply congratulated for having died while he was on in years but before suffering the infirmities of old age (*Evagoras* 71).

PATRIOTIC HISTORY

Depicting one's birthplace favorably was also a type of ethical history. Just as the historian was to judge the moral worth of the persons in his writings, so the reader would judge the moral worth of the historian. Hence the historian must endeavor to show himself to be grateful to those persons and institutions that had benefited him in his life, such as family, friends and country. To fail to to so, to cast them in an unflattering light or actually to criticize them, was to demonstrate a serious imperfection in character. Hence we find even such a stickler for historical truth as Polybius conceding that the historian should show partiality toward his native city provided that he does not contradict the facts (16.14). He criticizes Timaeus, however, for claiming that Sicily was better than the rest of Greece and Syracuse better than any city anywhere; Sicilian affairs were a mere tempest in a tea cup, Polybius says (12.23, 26b).

Local histories by their very nature would present the legends, institutions and history of a city in a favorable light, although they need not have been falsified or even much exaggerated. The history of his native Cyme, however, presented Ephorus with a challenge. It was not a large or important town, and was saddled with the reputation for stupidity (the town crier advised the inhabitants to take shelter when it rained, we hear: Strabo 13.3.6). Ephorus maintained that it was the birthplace of Homer and Hesiod, among other distinctions (*FGrH* 70 F1), and referred to it frequently in his history. Unfortunately, for long stretches nothing of much importance happened in Cyme; undaunted, Ephorus would add to his account of great events elsewhere, "During this same period the people of Cyme were at peace" (*FGrH* 70 F236).

"TRAGIC" HISTORY

During the Hellenistic age a style of writing arose that has been dubbed "tragic" because the aim of the historian was to recreate scenes of such vividness that they seemed to be happening before the readers' eyes, as if on a stage. The aim was to rouse the emotions, especially pity and fear, on beholding the protagonists buffeted by calamities and beset by twists of fate; the result was the pleasurable sense of being drawn into the drama of history and of experiencing vicariously the perils of the dramatis personae.

Much effort has been made to provide this style of writing with a theoretical underpinning, particularly from the school of Aristotle. That philosopher's discussion of tragedy in his *Poetics* is well known: the aim of tragedy, he said, was to produce pleasure (*hêdonê*) in the spectator through pity and fear arising out of the representation (*mimêsis*) of pitiful and fearful actions. Yet it is doubtful whether "tragic" history was the product of such theorizing. After all, gripping realism and high drama are to be found in Herodotus and Thucydides, both of whom were clearly influenced by the Attic stage. Later in antiquity Thucydides was held up as the master par excellence of this type of writing (e.g. Plutarch, *Moralia* 347 A–C). In the fourth century and Hellenistic age this approach to history became ever more popular, and was sometimes carried to extremes. The austere Thucydides had rejected mere entertainment as a goal of serious history: enlightenment was his aim, for all the drama and emotionalism of certain parts of his narrative. Some of his successors, however, seem to have regarded pleasure as their chief goal, and in this respect they struck out on a new path.

The chief exponent of this approach was Duris of Samos, a contemporary of Timaeus. In addition to his histories, Duris wrote works on Homer, tragedy, painting and sculpture. He made this pronouncement: "Ephorus and Theopompus failed for the most part to do justice to events. For neither dramatic representation (*mimêsis*) nor pleasure (*hêdonê*) have a place in their writing; they were only concerned with getting words down on paper" (*FGrH* 76 F1). It is a shame that we do not have enough left of Duris to say just how he embodied this credo in his own histories (it is worth noting that Cicero characterized him as "a conscientious historian:" *Letters to Atticus* 6.1.18). The fragments reveal a full-blown, ornamented style, while his works on tragedy and painting suggest a keen interest in drama and the visual arts, which some of the fragments bear out. Duris

119

was fond of elaborate tableaux, with special attention to costumes, colors, scents and sounds (e.g. *FGrH* 76 FF10, 14, 46).

With his successor and continuator, Phylarchus, we have more to go on, although some of the material has been transmitted through the prejudiced eyes of Polybius. In a long critique of Phylarchus' failings (2.56–63) Polybius complains particularly of the pathetic scenario that the historian gave when describing the capture of the city of Mantinea, including clinging women with hair dishevelled and breasts bared, throngs of men and women weeping as they are led off into captivity together with children and aged parents. Polybius says that Phylarchus' aim was to fill the reader with pity and that this was his goal throughout his history: he writes like a tragic poet, not a historian, in trying to shock and amaze. Yet there is a world of difference between the two genres, Polybius affirms, and he goes on to specify the differences (2.56). There is no reason to doubt Polybius' report of the way Phylarchus described the fall of Mantinea. But when we consider that the suffering of the inhabitants had been caused by Polybius' fellow Achaeans, we may suspect that it was not just Phylarchus' sensationalist writing that irked him. Polybius insists that the Mantineans received kind and humane treatment from the Achaeans when the latter garrisoned their town (2.57), and when the garrison was murdered and the town recaptured, "Nothing worse befell the Mantineans than the plunder of their property and the selling of their free citizens into slavery" (2.58). We hear of one episode in Phylarchus that replicated a complete tragic plot. According to myth, the husband of Eriphyle was warned he would die if he joined the expedition of the Seven Against Thebes, but she, bribed with a necklace by the leader of the expedition, persuaded her husband to go. He did so, but with foreboding, calling on his sons to kill Eriphyle should he perish. Perish he did, and the sons killed their mother. This was a well-known tragic subject; Sophocles wrote an *Eriphyle*, for example. In the fourth century BC the supposed necklace was on display in the temple of Athena at Delphi. Phylarchus told how, in the Sacred War of the 350s and 340s, an adulterous wife induced her paramour to loot Delphi and secure the necklace for her. He did so, but her younger son went mad and set the house on fire; she then perished in the conflagration wearing the fatal necklace (*FGrH* 81 F70).

Over a hundred years after Polybius, Dionysius of Halicarnassus in a literary letter to his friend Gnaeus Pompeius Geminus (3) compared Herodotus and Thucydides according to the following six requirements for good history. The first is to choose a noble subject that is pleasing to the reader. Herodotus wrote of Greece's glorious defeat of Persia, whereas Thucydides deliberately chose "a repellent and unfortunate war, which best of all, should not have happened, or (failing that) should have been consigned to silence and oblivion, and ignored by posterity." The second is to determine where to begin and how far to go. Herodotus was excellent on this score, but Thucydides began "when things started to go badly for Greece." His exile made him hostile to his native city, which he found responsible for the war's outbreak. Dionysius then gives a brief sketch of how Thucydides might have written his first book in order to shift the blame onto Sparta; moreover, he should have opened his work by describing Athens' glorious record in the aftermath of the Persian conflict "with patriotic fervor." As it was, he mentioned this period later in his first book in a brief and perfunctory flashback. The third task of a historian is to determine what events to include and which to omit. Herodotus, in imitation of Homer, included many engaging digressions, whereas Thucydides described battle upon battle with scarcely any relief, exhausting the reader's mind. The fourth criterion is to so arrange the material that every item is in its proper place. Herodotus here followed a natural order of events, with pleasing flashbacks and a sequence that is easy to follow. Thucydides, on the other hand, divided up the narrative by summers and winters, which, since events are going on in many theatres at once, required him to break off each story at the end of one season and resume it in the next. The fifth criterion concerns the attitude of the historian to his subject. "Herodotus' attitude is fair throughout, showing pleasure in the good and grief at the bad. That of Thucydides, on the other hand, is outspoken and harsh, and he bears a grudge against his country because of his exile." The final criterion concerns style; here Dionysius divides the prize between them, different though their styles are.

Dionysius' remarks date to the Roman period when classicism was in the ascendant (which Dionysius did much to promote). Moreover, he does not bother to justify these six criteria, claiming, rather disingenuously, that they are "what we look for in all histories." Then again, he gives the palm to Herodotus on all counts save the last, in this showing partiality to his fellow townsman. Yet at bottom these criteria are clearly an inheritance from the Hellenistic age, with their emphasis on pleasure, style, moral sensibility and patriotism. Above all, they derive from that school of historiography that regarded the writing of history as an artistic endeavor and the finished product as a literary artifact. There is not a word here about accuracy, research, truth, insight, impartiality or utility, to pick a half dozen other criteria. If Polybius could have read this passage of Dionysius, it would have brought on an apoplectic fit (after recovering from which he doubtless would have composed a trenchant and lengthy refutation). For Polybius belonged to a quite different school of historiography, as the final chapter will show.

7

POLYBIUS

Polybius of Megalopolis wrote a history of the Mediterranean world in forty books, covering the period 264–145 BC. The first two, which he characterizes as a "preparatory introduction" (*prokataskeuê*, 1.3), sketch events from the point where Timaeus' history had stopped, the outbreak of Rome's first war with Carthage in 264, to the beginning of the 140th Olympiad in 220 BC, shortly before the start of the second war with Carthage, which Rome fought against Hannibal. The main period covered in the history begins with Book 3. Its chief theme was Rome's expansion eastward and westward; Spain and parts of North Africa fell under her sway, while all the Hellenistic kingdoms were either annexed or controlled by those who ruled on Rome's sufferance.

Polybius was born around 200 BC into one of the leading families of the Achaean League in the Peloponnesus. His father Lycortas had been the annually elected general of the league more than once; the young Polybius was chosen in 182 BC to carry to burial the ashes of the most prominent Achaean leader in the second century, Philopoemen, "the last of the Greeks." In 170–169 Polybius was the league's cavalry commander, second in command to the general himself. This came at a critical moment, for Rome was at war with Perseus of Macedon and suspected that many states in Greece were secret sympathizers of the king. In this delicate situation the league tried to preserve its autonomy, but after Perseus' defeat at the Battle of Pydna in 168 Rome was in no mood to forgive those who had been neutral or who had adopted a posture of independence rather than giving her their wholehearted support. In consequence, one thousand Achaeans were brought in 167 to Rome for "questioning," but were kept for the next seventeen years as hostages for the league's good behavior. Polybius was among them. By a lucky accident he became acquainted with the young Scipio Aemilianus through the loan of some books (31.23) and because of this connection was able to remain in Rome while most of his fellow Achaeans were interned in various small towns in central Italy. As their friendship grew, Polybius became a mentor to the younger man, a scion of two of Rome's greatest patrician houses. First, he was the son of Aemilius Paullus, the man who had defeated King Perseus; Scipio had accompanied his father eastwards and had fought at Pydna. Second, he had been adopted into the family of the Cornelii Scipiones, thereby becoming the grandson of Scipio Africanus, the victor over Hannibal. Another of his brothers was adopted into another great patrician family, the Fabii (adoption as a way of continuing the family line was a common practice among the Roman nobility).

Polybius therefore had the opportunity to become acquainted with the nature of Roman politics and warfare first-hand and at the highest level; moreover, despite his status as an internee he enjoyed considerable freedom of action and movement. He tells us he encouraged and aided in the escape from Rome of the Seleucid Prince Demetrius, the future Demetrius I, a hostage like himself (31.11–15)—doubtless with the blessing of members of the Scipionic family. Polybius was able to undertake a number of journeys as well: to the toe of Italy on several occasions (12.5) and with Scipio to Africa, Spain and southern Gaul; he tells us he personally retraced Hannibal's route over the Alps into Italy "in order to learn the truth and see with my own eyes" (3. 48, 57–59).

In 150 BC Polybius and his fellow hostages (only three hundred were still surviving) received permission to return to Greece, but not before Cato the Censor said he thought debating whether a bunch of geriatric Greeks should be buried by Italian or Achaean undertakers a waste of the senate's time (35.6). Polybius found a hostile atmosphere back in Greece, where anti-Roman sentiment was strong and Roman apologists such as himself were unwelcome. Radical politicians led the Achaean League, whom Polybius loathed and distrusted (38.3, 10–13, 16, 18). By 146 BC he had joined Scipio in Africa, who was prosecuting Rome's third and last war against Carthage, and he witnessed the razing of that city to the ground. It was probably shortly afterwards that Polybius made a voyage into the Atlantic to explore the coastline of Morocco to the south and that of Portugal northwards (3.59, 34.15). In this same period a second and greater disaster struck. The Achaean League became embroiled in war with Rome and, on being defeated, its chief city Corinth was destroyed and its inhabitants enslaved. Polybius rushed back to Greece and worked hard to secure as favorable terms as he could (39.5), in appreciation for which decrees of thanks were voted and statues erected in many places (39.3). Polybius' whereabouts in the next years is uncertain; he paid one or more visits to Rome and was perhaps with Scipio during the siege and fall of the city of Numantia in Spain (133 BC). He also visited Alexandria in Egypt in this period (34.14). A late and not very reliable source says that he died at the age of eighty-two from a fall off a horse, which suits what is known of his active nature and love of horsemanship. The last datable event in his history is 118 BC (3.39).

Polybius wrote an encomiastic biography of Philopoemen, a treatise on military tactics and a monograph on the Numantine War, all of which are lost. He originally ended his history with the defeat of King Perseus and the settlement of Greece in 167 BC (Books 1–29). But when Rome simultaneously defeated Carthage and his own Achaean League—marked by the destruction of Carthage and Corinth in the single year 146—he decided to add eleven more books in a revised edition in order to bring down the narrative to include these momentous events (3.1–5); he also inserted a few new passages into the books he had already written. The first five books survive complete. The rest are represented mostly by excerpts, some quite extensive, made in the Byzantine period. It has been estimated that about thirty percent of the whole survives; Book 6 is nearly complete, Book 12 about half so, but others are quite fragmentary. For certain ones (17, 19, 26, 37 and 40) next to nothing survives because the books themselves had been lost by the tenth century when the excerpts were made. The regular narrative ended with Book 39. The last contained a chronological summary and an outline of the contents. If the history were fully extant, it would have been about five times the length of Thucydides.

Beginning with the regular part of his history in Book 3 Polybius adopts the Olympiad system of dating that Timaeus had introduced into history. He gives all events throughout the Mediterranean for each Olympiad year before beginning another, but does not follow the system rigidly. This is because the Olympiad year began in midsummer and hence required breaking the account of each campaigning season into two halves. Polybius regularly continues his account of military operations into the next Olympiad year in order not to leave the story unfinished. Within the Olympiad year he divides up the narrative into several theatres of operation, moving clockwise around the Mediterranean and treating each in this order: Italy (along with Sicily, Spain and North Africa), Greece and Macedon, Asia, Egypt. This occasionally results in awkwardness. For example, an embassy from Greece can arrive in Rome and transact its business before the notice of its dispatch is related, since affairs in Italy precede those of Greece (28.16). But Polybius alerts the reader to potentially confusing deviations, and he claims that this system of rotation adds variety and interest to his narrative (38.5–6).

Polybius announces the subject of his history in the form of a question:

> Who is so lacking in curiosity and so shiftless as not to wish to know by what means and under what kind of constitution in not quite fifty-three years the Romans conquered the entire inhabited world and subjected it to their sole rule—an event unique in history?
>
> (1.1)

He goes on to argue that none of the great empires of the past— Persian, Spartan or Macedonian—was as extensive as the Roman: "They have left as a legacy an empire that has no equal in the past and will have no rival in the future" (1.2). This achievement Polybius attributes to the work of Fortune or *Tyche*, and he uses metaphors from the stage to describe it: "*Tyche* is forever producing something new and forever playing a role in the lives of men, but she has never performed or put on such as showpiece as she has in our time" (1.4). Up to the start of the 140th Olympiad in 220 BC history had been a series of disconnected events, he argues, separate in their origins and effects. But after this point the ascendancy of Rome gathered all these disparate threads together and created a unified whole (1.3–4). This organic unity is the defining characteristic of Polybius' claim to be writing "universal" history, which none of his contemporaries had tried; he praises Ephorus as his first and only predecessor in taking such an approach (5.33).

Polybius is writing chiefly for a Greek audience, as is shown by his frequent remarks on Greek internal affairs and on the need for his countrymen to learn more about Rome and the West. Most particularly, he wants them to understand that Rome's success was due to her admirable customs and institutions, which he endeavors at many points in the history to explain, and to which he devotes the whole of Book 6. To a lesser extent he has Roman readers in mind also, for some of his comments are directed to them (e.g. 31.22). His audience will benefit from the study of his history, he says, in two ways (1.1): first, it will train and educate those engaged in political life and those eager to learn about it; second, it will help the general reader to endure the vicissitudes of fortune as he learns how others reacted to the pressures of success or failure.

Polybius' concern with the general reader is sporadic, though his view is consistent. He believes that how a man reacts to the vagaries of fortune reveals his true character and that learning through historical examples will show how best to handle crises (1.35 is especially clear on this). Since Fortune or *Tyche* is unstable by nature, moderation should be maintained in the face of success, as Scipio Africanus did (10.40); and in the face of adversity keeping a level head is important, which Hannibal exemplified in defeat (15.15–16). In fact, Polybius features the comments of both men on the nature of *Tyche* when they met on the eve before their final confrontation (15.6, 8). To be ever aware of the changeability of Fortune is a mark of a man's humanity and greatness. Polybius tells how Scipio Aemilianus burst into tears on seeing Carthage put to the torch, telling Polybius he feared his own city might someday suffer the same fate: "He could not have uttered a more profound or statesmanlike sentiment" (38.21). Groups and states will also learn how to bear up under misfortunes as well: for example, the Celts have terrorized many parts of the Mediterranean, Polybius says, but their attacks are disorganized and can be repulsed:

> I think history has a special obligation to record such episodes in the drama of Fortune and to pass them on to future generations so that those who come after us may not be wholly ignorant of them and may not be confounded by the sudden and unexpected inroads of these barbarians, but instead, having some appreciation of how short-lived and easily repulsed they are, may stand their ground under attack and do everything in their power not to yield to them in any way.
>
> (2.35)

Polybius' chief concern, however, is with the active or aspiring statesman, who will learn from history both practical lessons and general wisdom. On the practical side, Polybius' text will describe step-by-step techniques that the statesman may apply to everyday situations he is likely to encounter: for example, an up-to-date system of fire-signalling that Polybius himself helped to devise (10.43–47), or the importance of having scaling ladders of sufficient height to reach the tops of walls (5.98, 9.18). In short, "If you take from history its capability of giving practical instruction, what is left is utterly unexceptional and has nothing to teach us" (12.25g). History will also provide the statesman with more general knowledge: for example, how to find allies and supporters when on the defensive, how to coordinate one's forces in an offensive action and how to maintain support for one's policies and keep the status quo (3.12, 31). On a broader and deeper level, history will impart an understanding of political constitutions: how the different types work and what their strong and weak points are. It will also teach the importance of a nation's values and habits of thought, for until the statesman under-stands such matters he cannot deal with foreign powers as a diplomat or military commander with full success. Polybius styles the sort of history that will benefit the statesman and the student of politics as *pragmatikê*, or "pragmatic," by which he means political and military history. He differentiates it from those that featured myths, legends, genealogies and the foundations of cities and colonies (9.1–2), and contrasts it with the works of those historians who wrote in an exaggerated or sensationalist fashion, such as Phylarchus, who con-founded the quite different genres of history and tragedy (2.56), and with still others who related marvels (3.47–48), or told stories fit for children (16.12: Theopompus is named) or included material on a level with barbershop gossip (3.20).

In Polybius, didacticism is pronounced. Since his readers will gain immediate and long-range benefits, both of practical application and in general knowledge, they must know what he is about, what the lessons are and where to find them in his lengthy opus. His method is like that of the American drill sergeant in addressing recruits: "First I tell them what I'm going to tell them, then I tell them, then I tell them what I've told them." Polybius is forever signposting his narrative, giving notice where he is going, recapitulating and making back references; the entire last book was devoted to a geographical overview and an elaborate table of contents. He is in the habit of breaking into the narrative frequently to give instruction on all manner of subjects: one geographical excursus begins with the points of the compass and builds up from there (3.36); another discourses on the utility of music in promoting civilized behavior (4.20–21); still another gives pointers for successful pig farming (12.4). In Book 36 (12) he interrupts to say that the frequent references to himself have been necessitated by his personal involvement in many of the events he describes, but that he has varied these personal intrusions (by using

"Polybius, I, we," etc.) in order to avoid seeming self-centered. He even interrupts to explain in three chapters why he is not now interrupting his narrative with yet another digression (3.57–59). Polybius is not an allusive writer: he articulates the lessons he wishes his readers to learn, even when they are obvious. These, as he concedes on occasion, may be dry and may be thought unnecessary; but they *are* necessary if one is to derive the full benefit of his message.

Truth for Polybius is the *sine qua non* of history. The reason is obvious: if history is to convey practical instruction and useful political precepts, it must be accurate. Truth is to history, he says on two occasions, what eyesight is to a living creature; if you take truth away, all that remains is a story without value (1.14, 12.12). Not only that, it has the potential to be positively harmful should someone try to model his conduct and policies on untruthful accounts. This is perhaps the most most important reason for his frequent and lengthy criticisms of other historians. They do not understand the serious purpose of history; they exaggerate, they embroider, they falsify. He objects to those like Phylarchus who wrote in the "tragic" mode because they indulged in melodrama and pandered to debased tastes. Others, like Timaeus, inserted speeches at every opportunity, putting words in the speakers' mouths that they never said and never would have said (12.25a–b, i–26c). Speeches are an essential part of history, Polybius affirms, but the reader must know what the actual arguments were in order to learn why some led to success and others to failure. From such awareness we can better calculate the sort of thing we should imitate and avoid (12.25a–b). The upshot is that the historian has the obligation to report what was actually said, however commonplace (2.56; cf. 29.12, 36.1). Polybius' concern for the truth led him at one point to write to a contemporary historian, Zeno of Rhodes, in order to point out some mistakes Zeno had made, "not to enhance one's own reputation by pointing out the mistakes of others, as some people do, but to look to the future and correct one's own mistakes and those of others to benefit the world at large" (16.20). Zeno, says Polybius, "gave a friendly reception to my comments" but pointed out that since his history had already been published, corrections to what was now in the public domain were no longer possible.

On a more practical level, Polybius critiques the knowledge of military matters shown by some of his predecessors. Ephorus gave commendable accounts of naval operations: "The reader quite rightly admires the historian for his ability and knowledge, and takes away much useful information that he can put to use in a similar situation" (12.25f). But Ephorus was quite deficient when it came to land battles (as were Theopompus and Timaeus): his accounts of the Battles of Leuctra (371 BC) and Mantinea (362 BC) made little sense given the topography and the number and movements of the troops. Callisthenes' description of the Battle of Issus in 333 BC in which Alexander defeated the forces of Darius III was similarly deficient, says Polybius in a long critique, even though Callisthenes himself was present (12.17–22).

But it is Timaeus for whom he has the harshest words. Book 12 is devoted to an attack on him, in the course of which Polybius also refutes the criticisms that Timaeus had levelled at others, including Ephorus, Theopompus and Aristotle. He singles out three areas in which writers of political history (*pragmatikê historía*) must be proficient: the study of written sources, autopsy of the places one writes about and experience in political affairs (12.25e). Of these, Timaeus was conversant with only the first: "He fancied that by settling down in Athens for nearly fifty years and acquainting himself with what his predecessors had written, he had thoroughly prepared himself to write history—a quite deluded supposition in my view" (12.25d). A bit later (12.25h) Polybius represents Timaeus as "frankly admitting he had had no military experience of any sort and had never inspected the places [he wrote about]." Even so, the study of written documents is the least important of the three, Polybius maintains (12.25i); book learning cannot substitute for on-site inspection and involvement in political life. Hence Timaeus' history was lifeless and frequently in error because of his lack of experience. Just as you cannot cure a sick patient or steer a ship from books alone, Polybius says, you cannot write history from an armchair. He concedes that it is difficult for a man to be experienced in everything, but in the case of history, travel and participation in politics are essential. "It will be well with history," he writes (12.28), adapting Plato's words in the *Republic* (473C–E), "either when statesmen undertake to write history... or when those intending to do so regard direct involvement in political life as indispensable for the writing of history." It should be emphasized that Polybius was well acquainted with the works of other historians and with many other kinds of written sources, and went out of his way to track them down. For example, he personally discovered an inscription Hannibal set up at a temple on the coast in south Italy, specifying the number of troops and elephants he brought with him over the Alps (3.33, 56); he had in his possession a letter of Scipio

Africanus to Philip V, doubtless through the good offices of Scipio
Aemilianus (10.9); he discusses in detail three Roman treaties that had
only recently come to light (3.26), the first of which dated to the first
years of the Roman republic (ca. 500 BC) and was written in such
archaic Latin that it was exceedingly difficult to decipher (3.22).

Polybius himself had not only been involved in politics and
military life, but was famous for his extensive travels. An honorary
inscription set up in his native Megalopolis described him as one who
had "wandered over every land and sea" (Pausanias 8.30), the fruits of
which can be seen in Book 34, the whole of which was an excursus on
the geography of Europe and Africa. In support of the necessity for
personal investigation he quotes Ephorus, Theopompus and Homer
(12.27). The passages from Homer refer to the much-travelled
Odysseus: "I think that just this sort of man should write history."
It was doubtless this connection that Cato the Censor had in mind
when he wittily observed, after Polybius and the surviving Achaean
exiles had won their release and had entered the senate house a second
time to seek restoration of their former honors, that Polybius was
behaving like Odysseus going back into the Cyclop's cave to retrieve
the hat and belt he had left behind (35.6).

Polybius' insistence that autopsy and political experience are more
important than the study of written sources reflects his conviction that
contemporary history is the only kind of serious history and that
"personal inquiry is the most important means of doing it" (12.4c).
Accordingly, he says he chose a subject that coincided with his own
generation and that of his father:

> In consequence of which I was present myself at some events,
> while I heard from those who had been eyewitnesses in the case
> of others. To go further back in time would be to write hearsay
> based on hearsay, which seems to me a shaky basis for making
> judgments and assertions.
>
> (4.2)

In Book 9 he is equally emphatic: to write of genealogies, the founding
of cities, myths and such like (of which Timaeus made a specialty,
12.26d) means that the writer

> either must repeat what others have said, while passing it off as
> his own, which is most reprehensible, or, if he refuses to do this,
> his work will prove quite pointless, since he will perforce
> concede that what he writes and thinks about is what his

131

predecessors had adequately treated before.... Accordingly, it was my decision to write contemporary history, first because new events are constantly taking place and require treatment for the first time . . . and, second, because this is the most instructive kind of history of all.

(9.2)

By and large Polybius succeeded in writing truthful history. What can be cited against his veracity does not amount to much. He concedes that one should show favoritism to one's country, but only if it does not contradict the facts (16.14), and while he thinks that belief in religious miracles is a sign of a blunted intelligence, he argues that because stories of the supernatural contribute to the piety felt by ordinary people they can have a limited place in history (16.12) and that by promoting religious superstition statesmen can keep the restless masses under control (6.56; cf. 10.2). He shows a strong and persistent bias against the enemies of his own Achaean League, especially the Aetolians, who are constantly characterized as barbarous, perfidious and predatory (e.g. 2.45–46, 4.3, 4.67, 18.34). Occasionally he will adopt some of the trappings of "tragic" history, such as stressing the paradoxical and unexpected, or characterizing certain actions as striking, thrilling or suspenseful (e.g. 3.43, 18.35, 23.10–11). But he does not stoop to sensationalism; the infrequent "tragic" touches arise naturally from the situations he describes.

Despite minor lapses from the standard of strict veracity, it is clear that Polybius is writing in the tradition of Thucydides and is opposed to those for whom history was a vehicle for displaying their rhetorical virtuosity and for catering to the public's taste for the emotional and sensational. Both historians rejected the distant past as a fit subject for history, embracing contemporary history in its political and military aspects, and stressing that their information derived from their own observation and the testimony of eye-witnesses. Both emphasized the usefulness of their histories over against simple entertainment. Although Polybius admits that pleasure is a legitimate aim (e.g. 7.7, 15.36, 31.30), he says he made the austere choice to concentrate on a political theme and to forgo digressions concerning genealogies, myths and other antiquarian subjects that the majority of readers find appealing and diverting (9.1–2). Nor did he place a high value on distinguished style, as his Greek shows, which is wordy and pedestrian. He disparages those who exalt style above substance and says there are many qualities more important than style on which a historian should pride himself (16.17; cf. 29.12). He concedes that the public found his work hard to come by and daunting to read because of the length of the books and their number (3.32).

In addition to *pragmatikê historía*, or political-military history, to describe his special approach, Polybius also uses the term *apodeiktikê* —"detailed/explanatory" history—by which he means that events are fully described and reasons given for what transpired, and that causation is a chief concern (2.37, 3.31–32). He contrasts himself in this respect with historians who make unsupported assertions and with histories that, because of their narrow theme, are unable to trace cause and effect among the different theatres of operation throughout the Mediterranean world. He also contrasts *apodeiktikê historía* with the selective outline of events he gave in his "preparatory introduction" in Books 1 and 2. He signals the change almost at once by analyzing the causes of wars, using the conflict with Hannibal as his chief illustration and citing others for corroboration (3.6–31). He begins by objecting to historians who confuse the causes of wars with their first actions: that is, with the precipitating incidents. Causes he terms *aitiai*, precipitating incidents *archai*, while *prophasis* denotes the pretext or reason alleged by either or both sides, whether true or false. His terminology is at variance with that of Thucydides, who uses *aitiai* to denote grounds of complaint or grievances, which answer to Polybius' *archai*, while *alêthestatê prophasis* for Thucydides signifies the truest, or underlying, cause. Polybius' scheme is in implicit disagreement with Thucydides, whom he does not mention here; in fact he names him only once and in passing (8.11; he never mentions Herodotus).

Polybius first uses the war of Alexander against Persia to illustrate his scheme (3.6). The causes were two: the escape of the Ten Thousand from Persia under Xenophon and the operations that King Agesilaus carried out in Persian territory a few years later, from which Philip II saw that Persia was vulnerable and that the rewards of conquest would be great. Philip gave as a pretext that he was avenging the injuries done to the Greeks, while the precipitating incident was Alexander's crossing into Asia. Polybius' second illustration concerns the war Rome fought against the Seleucid king Antiochus III in the years 192–188 (3.7). The cause was the anger of the Aetolians, who thought Rome had not sufficiently rewarded them for their help in Rome's war against Philip V of Macedon (200–196 BC), and so urged on Antiochus and promised him their full support should he cross over into Greece. The pretext was the liberation of Greece, while the precipitating incident was Antiochus' landing on the Greek mainland. Finally, the war with Hannibal is explained as follows (3.9–10). The first cause was the wrath of Hannibal's father, Hamilcar, who resented the defeat of Carthage in the First Punic War (264–241 BC). The second was the anger engendered by Rome's unjust annexation of Sardinia and exaction of a large indemnity after the war, when Carthage was weak and in no position to resist (238 BC). The third cause was the subsequent success of the Carthaginians in Spain, whose money and manpower led to Carthage's remarkable recovery. After Hamilcar's death, his anger passed to his son-in-law Hasdrubal and then to Hannibal. The precipitating incidents were Hannibal's siege and capture of the city of Saguntum in Spain, which was an ally of Rome, and his crossing of the Ebro River, which by treaty marked the northern limit of Carthaginian control in Spain (Saguntum, however, was south of the Ebro). Finally, as a pretext Hannibal charged that the Romans had unjustly executed some of Saguntum's leading citizens and that he had been called in to avenge this wrong (3.15: a feeble pretext, says Polybius; he would have done better to have cited the seizure of Sardinia and the indemnity). Polybius then proceeds to give Rome's justification before finally debating which of the two sides should be charged with the responsibility (*aitia*, 3.28) of having started the war. He concludes that if Saguntum was the cause, Carthage was to blame, but if the seizure of Sardinia and the indemnity were, Rome was responsible (3.30).

All this is rather mechanical and somewhat disappointing, especially when compared with Thucydides. Polybius' concept of cause and effect is often one-sided, as we can see in the case of Carthage's success in Spain, which is cited as one of the three causes of the war; but there is no mention that this success must have increased Rome's fears and suspicions. Nor does he say what Antiochus' motive was in invading Greece, fixing only on the anger of the Aetolians. There is great emphasis also on individuals and on the transmission of emotions and intentions to successors, the effect sometime lasting for many years. Polybius wavers between citing states of mind as causes, such as anger and resentment, and particular incidents, such as the escape of the Ten Thousand, or overall results, such as Carthage's success in Spain. We would suppose that at bottom the mental and emotional reactions of individuals and groups to events are the real causes, although Polybius does not say so and his citation of new events and new reactions to events produces a rather fuzzy picture.

Ultimately, however, his schema is simplistic: it reduces causation to a formula and fails to account for the complex and dynamic interaction of events and states of mind. Furthermore, since he defines *aitiai* as those factors that shape our decisions in advance, he must first determine who did the deciding; this in turn prompts him to regard the issue as one of fixing blame or responsibility. We are not very far removed here from Herodotus' view of *aitiai*. It is puzzling, and doubtless for the best, that Polybius makes only partial and intermittent use of this scheme in discussing the causes of the other wars he describes in his history. Note, too, that, the formula *aitiai–prophasis–archai* does not explain why events other than wars occur.

Polybius' main thesis is that the rise of Rome was explicable in rational terms. Her foreign wars are described as resulting one from another in a progressive series (3.32). Furthermore, she consciously aimed at world domination: "It is quite natural that, having been schooled in such great enterprises, they not only boldly threw themselves into gaining the leadership and mastery of the world, but then succeeded in realizing their aims" (1.63). His explanation for Rome's appropriation of the gold and silver of Syracuse during the war with Hannibal is that "they could not lay claim to world power without taking away the resources of others and appropriating them for themselves" (9.10). Just what put this idea in the Romans' minds is not made clear; the acquisition of empire is a noble enterprise that seems to be a natural impulse, which in the case of the Romans was consciously carried out. Polybius praises them for being superior to the Spartans in that the latter were basically stay-at-homers and insufficiently aggressive, whereas the Romans aimed at power from the start and put all their energies into its attainment (6.50). Yet despite the thesis that Rome's expansion was consciously aggressive, Polybius' account of the events leading up to her many wars almost invariably places the blame for starting these conflicts on her enemies. This probably derives from the Roman credo that only just wars were permissable: that is, Rome must never be the aggressor. Another discrepancy appears when we try to reconcile the view that Rome's achievement was consciously pursued with the notion, mentioned earlier, that Fortune or *Tyche* was responsible for it (1.4). *Tyche* in this formulation seems equivalent to providence: some supernatural force has guided events to a predetermined end. Yet in many other places Polybius uses the word to mean simply accident or coincidence for which no rational explanation is apparent (cf. 36.17). So there is real ambiguity here. On the one hand, Polybius believes that Rome's success is fully explicable in rational terms; on the other, in some sense and at some other level her success was achieved under the guidance of *Tyche*, who was often spoken of as a goddess in the Hellenistic age.

Polybius devotes the whole of Book 6 to an analysis of the Roman constitution and of certain military and cultural practices that the discussion suggested to him. This was part of his plan from the very start: "Who [would] . . . not wish to know by what measures and under what kind of constitution in not quite fifty-three years the Romans conquered the entire inhabited world?" (1.1). He elected to place this discussion after Hannibal had dealt Rome the most crushing defeat in her history, the Battle of Cannae in 216 BC, in which one of the two consuls, over half the senate and some 70,000 soldiers perished (3.117: Books 4 and 5 complete his account of the 140th Olympiad with events in the East, 220–216 BC). Yet the Romans pulled themselves together after this disaster and by determination, skill and a unified effort were able to defeat Carthage in the end. Rome's constitution was in Polybius' view the most important factor in her victory over Hannibal and in the subsequent acquisition of her empire. Book 6 is therefore much more than a digression or excursus, for its subject lies at the heart of his interpretation of history.

Polybius outlines a cycle of constitutional changes that he styles *anacyclôsis* (6.5–9, a rare term in Greek). The initial phase occurs at a time when some great disaster has left men weak, disorganized and living in a state of savagery. A single strong individual emerges to coerce the people into obeying his dictates and ceasing to prey upon one another. This phase Polybius calls *monarchia*, during which men gradually develop a sense of duty and justice from the rearing of offspring, from whom they naturally expect gratitude and obedience. A sense of right and wrong thus arises, which lays the groundwork for the appearance of true kingship: as moral sensibility replaces physical coercion, the king rules with the willing support of his subjects. But his descendants, because of rank and privilege, begin to commit acts of violence against the citizenry and lose their support. Kingship thus gives way to tyranny, but when the tyrant's excesses become unendurable, the best men with the support of the masses drive him from power. Aristocracy begins; but their descendants succumb to the temptation of abusing their privileged position, as had the descendants of the king. As those in power lose support and tighten their grip, aristocracy develops into oligarchy, whose growing abuses trigger an uprising of the people and their overthrow. Democracy then holds sway, but the next generations become so accustomed to freedom and equality that they no long value them; the result is increasing violence, which leads democracy to metamorphose into ochlocracy or mob-rule. In the end anarchy prevails, and out of the chaos a strong monarch appears once more to initiate the cycle anew.

This cycle Polybius describes as occurring "in accordance with nature" (*physis*, 6.4, 9) and going through regular changes of growth and decay. The three simple forms of kingship, aristocracy and democracy have as their debased counterparts tyranny, oligarchy and ochlocracy. Monarchy is the catalyst that emerges from mob-rule and initiates kingship. Because the cycle is regular and inevitable, Polybius claims that once a person recognizes where a particular state is in the cycle, he can predict what the future holds for it (6.9).

Rome, however, along with certain other states whose constitutions he also discusses, had managed to achieve what he styles a mixture of these three basic constitutional forms, which played off against one another in such a way that the state was kept in a position of equilibrium and the change inherent in *anacyclôsis* was arrested (6.10). "Mixture" is therefore inaccurate: the three forms were not so much intermingled as counterbalanced. Sparta had achieved a mixed constitution through the wise foresight of a single lawgiver, Lycurgus. Rome, by contrast, had produced the same result through a natural political development in which experience gained through trial and error gradually led her to adopt an enviable mix of kingship, aristocracy and democracy. The mixed constitution does not arrest change permanently, however; sooner or later all such constitutions lose their equilibrium, as Rome's would do someday, and reenter the cycle of change that is *anacyclôsis* (6. 9–10, 51, 57). Polybius characterizes the mixed constitution of Carthage as having become unbalanced by the time of the war with Hannibal: the people had encroached on the power of deliberation that properly belonged to the Carthaginian council: hence Carthage was on the decline, losing its stability and slipping into the process of *anacyclôsis*, whereas Rome had kept the deliberative powers of the senate intact and was therefore at her acme (6.51).

Polybius identifies kingship with the two consuls, who possessed great power in their year of office; aristocracy with the senate, the only deliberative body that could give continuity to policy; and democracy with the popular assemblies, which elected the magistrates and voted all legislation. In a famous section (6.11–18) he describes the system of checks and balances that obtained among

137

consuls, senate and people, which prevented any one element from becoming preponderant.

Unfortunately the section in which Polybius described *anacyclôsis* in Rome's early history survives in only a few fragments. Yet something like the following reconstruction is probable. The regal period (traditional dates 753–509 BC) began with the formation of a new and undisciplined society under Romulus (=*monarchia*); kingship was realized under the first Tarquin and his successor Servius Tullius; while tyranny flourished in the reign of the second Tarquin, surnamed "the Proud," who was expelled along with his family in 509 by the leading senatorial families. The first years of the republic witnessed the ascendancy of aristocracy, while in the middle of the fifth century oligarchy appeared in the form of the evil decemvirs, who illegally tried to perpetuate their tenure of office (cf. 6.11). At their fall, the reestablishment of republican government under consuls, senate and assemblies marked the arresting of the *anacyclôsis* through the emergence of the mixed constitution, which grew in strength thereafter. The section on checks and balances follows (6.11–18).

Neither the conception of *anacyclôsis* nor that of the mixed constitution was original to Polybius; one can see elements of both in many writers (for example, Plato's *Republic* 8.544C and *Laws* 4.712D–E), although we nowhere encounter the overall scheme that Polybius presents in Book 6. Some refinements and emphases may well have been original to him, but exactly which ones is impossible to fix with certainty, given the nature of our sources. Polybius' discussion had a profound effect on political thought in the modern era, particularly the eighteenth century, including Montesquieu and the framers of the American Constitution.

In some respects Polybius' formulation of constitutional change is mechanical and simplistic; here, as in his discussion of causation, his commitment to a theory prevents him from appreciating the complexities of a particular historical process. On the other hand, there is much in Book 6 that is acutely observed. The excellence of a constitution, he argues, depends on a state's laws and customs: bad laws and bad habits will vitiate a constitution that is admirable in theory (6.47). In other words, the value of a constitution depends on the values of the people who live under it. Had Polybius pursued this idea further when discussing how the Roman constitution operated, he might have realized that so many possibilities for breakdown were inherent in it that the wonder is not that it worked well but that it worked at all.

When Polybius gets away from the straightjacket of theory, he comes into his own in a quite remarkable way. At least half of what survives from Book 6 concerns the military, social and religious practices of the Romans (19–42, 51–56, 58). Polybius is at pains to show his readers, particularly his Greek readers, just why the Romans had succeeded as completely and as brilliantly as they had. A long section on the military system (6.19–42) describes in painstaking detail subjects like recruitment, the organization of the army and cavalry, the building of a Roman camp, the chain of command, the movement of troops, pay scales, punishments and rewards. The passage is a tour de force in its way, for as the details pile up, the sheer doggedness and power of the Romans comes through in a manner that no generalized description could ever convey. The resulting picture is of a huge and well-oiled machine, fueled by hard work, strict obedience to orders and by every man knowing his place and duties. From his description one understands not just how the military worked (which Polybius was keenly interested in for its own sake) or why it was so successful, but what kind of communal cooperation underlay the working of the constitution itself.

In a somewhat later section (6.51–56) he compares Carthage with Rome more on the basis of their habits and values than of their constitutions per se, before going on to commend the Romans both for their honesty in money matters and for scrupulous concern for religion (6.56: he believes this shows their desire to keep the masses in check). But the most remarkable passage comes in his description of the funeral of a Roman noble (6.53–54). His aim here is to illustrate how the Roman sees his own good as subsumed in the greater good of family and nation and that in contemplating the achievements of his ancestors he is inspired to add to the glory of family and country by his own exploits. In the entrance hall of every noble house the death masks of all the male ancestors were on display. When a man died, various dependents of the household took the masks down, put them on and dressed themselves in the robes of the highest office that each ancestor had held in his lifetime. The deceased was dressed in his highest robes also and was carried out of the house to a public spot such as the forum, followed by his ancestors, each in a chariot and accompanied by people on foot dressed as the officials who had once attended him by right of his having been a magistrate. The corpse was displayed on a platform, propped up and facing the crowd, while his ancestors took their places around him. A family member would then deliver a speech on the exploits of both the deceased and the ancestors present. Who would not be moved by such as sight, Polybius asks. And indeed it must have presented an uncanny spectacle: on that day the dead reappeared on earth, looking and moving as they had in life.

As remarked before, the mixed constitution can maintain its existence for only a limited time. Sooner or later the balance will be upset and *anacyclôsis* will resume its course. Rome is no exception: in several places Polybius anticipates the time when this must happen. In giving his reasons for adding Books 30–40 to the previously completed books he says that contemporary readers, from learning of the period 167–145 BC, will now be able to judge for themselves whether Roman rule was to be regretted or welcomed, and future generations whether it was worthy of praise or blame, based on an assessment of how the Romans used their power (3.4). In the public sphere, he records a whole series of cynical actions, particularly on the part of the senate, but without criticizing any of them. For example, when King Eumenes of Pergamum, an ally of Rome, sent his brother Attalus to Rome in 168/167 as his envoy, certain Romans tried to undermine his loyalty to Eumenes; when this failed, the senate reneged on its promise to award certain territories to Pergamum (30.1–3). And when Eumenes a bit later came to pay a visit in person, he was turned away at his place of disembarkation and sent home in humiliation; the senate, says Polybius, hoped the Galatians, Eumenes' enemies, would take this as encouragement to attack him (30.19). Many examples of similar conduct in these years could be cited from what is left of Books 30 and following. In the private sphere, Polybius is openly critical of some of the youth in matters of sex and luxurious living, and in a lengthy passage contrasts their conduct with the high principles and self-restraint of Scipio Aemilianus (31.25–29).

Except for his criticism of these anonymous young nobles, Polybius does not give his own assessment of the worth of Roman behavior in this period. Why was this? One explanation is that Polybius thought Rome was justified in her new ruthlessness: this was how an imperial power kept her subjects under her thumb. Certainly Polybius is generally unsympathetic to the losers in history; success was what counted, and success he tended to equate with moral worth. Even so, if he saw nothing objectionable in Rome's new style of diplomacy, why did he ask the question whether Rome's empire was to be regretted or welcomed only to leave it unanswered? Certainly he is not shy elsewhere in airing his views or telling his readers what lessons his narrative holds for them. At 9.10 he asks whether the Romans in 211

BC were justified in confiscating the art treasures of Syracuse and carrying them off to Rome, and proceeds to give the unequivocal answer of no. One might argue that so much of the last books has been lost that, although he gave an opinion, it no longer survives. But the very idea that he gave one may be doubted. On the one hand, it is difficult to see why, if he himself judged Roman rule to be welcome and anticipated posterity's positive verdict, he would not have said so in the passages we have. On the other, if he were inclined to be negative, he would have found himself in a delicate and potentially embarrassing position, for he surely would have been reluctant to offend his Roman friends whom he admired, especially Scipio Aemilianus. This, I suggest, is probably where the answer lies. The historian, usually so free in stating his opinions, finds himself in the last books under unaccustomed constraint. He therefore invites readers and posterity to deliver the verdict he could not give himself.

A slight but palpable pall of disillusion thus descends over Polybius' last books. One final contrast should be noted. In describing why the mixed constitution begins to decline in a flourishing state, he singles out extravagance, the ostentatious display of wealth and competition for honors as the consequences of prosperity (6.57), and in describing Rome's behavior after the fall of the Macedonian monarchy, he notes that the enormous influx of wealth from Macedon into Rome led to extravagance, luxury and the idle parade of riches (31.25). The similarity between the two passages is striking, and it is not difficult to see what conclusion the alert reader was expected to draw.

EPILOGUE

Most historians discussed in this book suffered exile or separation from their native cities at some point in their lives, a phenomenon that did not go unnoticed by the ancients (Plutarch, *Moralia* 605C). Certainly Herodotus, Thucydides, Xenophon and Polybius fall into this category, as do many of the fragmentary historians, such as Philistus, Theopompus and Timaeus. All had been involved in political life and had left their native cities for political reasons. In exile the writing of history proved an outlet for their interest in politics, and by becoming acquainted with foreign places and peoples they acquired a broader and more ecumenical outlook than might have been the case if they had stayed at home; and, of course, they enjoyed access to information from a wide spectrum of sources, sometimes from former enemies, which gave them (or at least some of them) a perspective and detachment that served them well as historians. Contact with non-Greek peoples was an especially strong stimulus to write history, such as Persia in the case of Herodotus, Ctesias, Xenophon and certain of the Alexander historians, and Rome in the case of Polybius. The contrast with barbarian societies helped to define their sense of Greekness and to situate Hellenism in the politics and culture of the Mediterranean world at large.

Almost all Greek historians down to the age of Polybius were concerned with contemporary history or near-contemporary history: that is, with events that fell in their own lifetimes or in the preceding generation. Even the few histories that began in the distant past, such those of Ephorus and Philistus, brought the narrative down to the present, which received the greatest emphasis and the most extensive treatment. City histories, too, with their accounts of foundings, myths and genealogies, came down to the lifetime of the author. Polybius' remarks make clear why this was so (9.2): to write the history of earlier

142

times was essentially to recast in one's own words what others had already done. The past when viewed from this perspective was a known quantity. One could not hope to add much new information to it, given the fact that the subject matter of history was essentially what people had said and done; only the testimony of eyewitnesses and the recollections of contemporaries could shed fresh light on these subjects. Moreover, the truth about the remote past was suspect because there was no way to crosscheck it, and the further back one went, the greater the uncertainty. Even Ephorus, who began his *Hellenica* with events of the eleventh century, affirmed this general proposition (*FGrH* 70 F9). But a historian of talent and ambition would not make his chief aim the correction of someone else's narrative when he could make his name by writing contemporary history. Thus Polybius did not go back to redo what his bête noire Timaeus had already done, even though Timaeus had done much of it badly, if we are to believe Polybius. This is why historians regularly begin their works at a point where significant predecessors had stopped. For example, Polybius continued Timaeus' work in his "preparatory introduction" (Books 1 and 2); for the regular part of his history beginning in 220 BC he picked up the narrative where the memoirs of the Achaean statesman Aratus had ended (1.3).

One should stress that the remote past was not deemed unhistorical or an unfit subject for history. As noted in the first chapter, the heroes of mythology were believed to have been real and the great events of legend to have happened. Callisthenes, for example, though a writer of contemporary history, could in an aside unblushingly fix the month and day for the fall of Troy (*FGrH* 124 F10a). And Polybius could, in quoting Homer on the travels of Odysseus, hold him up as a model for would-be historians to follow, such as the inert Timaeus. What people found objectionable in myth and legend were the improbabilities. To retail miracles, fantastic occurrences and impossible scenarios was a sign of naivety and childishness. Herodotus suffered from this stigma throughout antiquity (and into modern times). Josephus in the first century AD remarked that "Ephorus accuses Hellanicus of lying, Timaeus accuses Ephorus and later writers accuse Timaeus; but absolutely everybody accuses Herodotus of it" (*Against Apion* 1.16). To describe persons and events from myth and legend was, if not the mark of a great historian, at least an acceptable procedure, provided it was done in a realistic and believable manner.

Most historians were thus reluctant to make their main task the retelling of what others had already done. But by way of compensation

143

they could, through various asides and digressions, censure and correct selectively. This is probably the most important reason for there being a tradition in historiography of criticizing one's predecessors. One could set the record straight on at least a limited number of topics in past history and still do justice to the central task of narrating present-day events. Such criticism served, of course, to highlight one's own high standards. At the very start Hecataeus criticized the silly stories of the Greeks, while Herodotus attacked Hecataeus, and Thucydides Herodotus. The chain continued unbroken to Polybius, with only Xenophon standing outside the tradition. But the habit grew exponentially and almost got out of hand. Timaeus was so free in his criticisms of just about everybody that he was wittily dubbed Epitimaeus: Mr Faultfinder. The man who coined this epithet, Ister of Cyrene, composed a critique of Timaeus that ran to at least two books, while Polemon of Troy followed with a tract entitled *Against Timaeus* in twelve volumes. Polybius' single book on the subject seems skimpy by comparison.

After Polybius Greek historiography began to lose many of its characteristic features. Contemporary histories became less popular; in their place epitomes and synoptic works grew in favor. Diodorus Siculus, for example, wrote his *Historical Library* in the last half of the first century BC, condensing all of Greek and Roman history from mythological times to his own day into forty books, the same number that Polybius had needed to narrate the events of 130 years. One reason for the declining popularity of contemporary history was the inhibition that people felt in expressing their honest opinions. Under Hellenistic monarchs and Roman emperors open criticism of those in power was unsafe, while praise could be interpreted as a sign of servility and dependence. I suggested in the last chapter that such wariness can be glimpsed in Polybius' last books, in which he does not express his own opinion on whether Roman rule was to be regretted or welcomed, but leaves the reader to decide. And in a significant passage in Book 8 (8) he frankly admits that the objective bestowal of praise and blame on monarchs is not always possible for the historian, although it should always be his goal. This dampening effect on free speech also affected criticism of one's predecessors, which became less frequent after Polybius. As a result, some in time came to believe that history of the past was a better thing than contemporary history. The veracity of the latter could be compromised by the bias felt toward the living autocrat and his ministers; but if the historian chose to write of bygone eras, he could freely express what he thought and felt,

144

unaffected by fear or favoritism: this is Diodorus' claim, for example (14.1, 15.1). Truth when viewed from this perspective is basically a negative concept: when you remove the bias that fear or flattery of the powerful engenders, truth is the residuum. A great sea change thus came over the writing of history by the Greeks, a reflection of the new political realities of the Mediterranean world.

FURTHER READING

For those interested in books devoted to individual historians, I would suggest Gould for Herodotus, Finley for Thucydides, Dillery for Xenophon and Walbank for Polybius.

GENERAL

Brown, T.S. (1973) *The Greek Historians*, Lexington MA: D.C. Heath & Co.
Bury, J.B. (1909) *The Ancient Greek Historians*, London: Macmillan & Co.
Collingwood, R.G. (1946) *The Idea of History*, Oxford: Oxford University Press.
Fornara, C.W. (1983) *The Nature of History in Ancient Greece and Rome*, Berkeley and Los Angeles: University of California Press.

BEFORE HISTORY

Jaeger, W. (1944) *Paideia: The Ideals of Greek Culture*, 3 vols, transl. G. Highet, New York: Oxford University Press.
Pearson, L. (1939) *Early Ionian Historians*, Oxford: Oxford University Press.

HERODOTUS

Benardete, S. (1969) *Herodotean Inquiries*, The Hague: Martinus Nijhoff.
Fornara, C.W. (1971) *Herodotus: An Interpretive Essay*, Oxford: Oxford University Press.
Gould, J. (1989) *Herodotus*, New York: St Martin's Press.
Hartog, F. (1988) *The Mirror of Herodotus*, transl. J. Lloyd, Berkeley and Los Angeles: University of California Press.
Herodotus and the Invention of History (1987) vol. 20 of *Arethusa*, Buffalo NY.
Hunter, V. (1982) *Past and Process in Herodotus and Thucydides*, Princeton: Princeton University Press.
Immerwahr, H. (1966) *Form and Thought in Herodotus*, Cleveland: American Philological Association.

Lateiner, D. (1989) *The Historical Method of Herodotus*, Toronto: University of Toronto Press.
Redfield, J. (1985) "Herodotus the Tourist," in *Classical Philology* 80: 97–118.
Ste Croix, G.E.M. de (1977) "Herodotus," *Greece and Rome* 24: 130–148.

THUCYDIDES

Cochrane, C.N. (1929) *Thucydides and the Science of History*, Oxford: Oxford Univeristy Press.
Connor, W.R. (1984) *Thucydides*, Princeton: Princeton University Press.
Cornford, F.M. (1907) *Thucydides Mythistoricus*, London: Routledge & Kegan Paul.
Edmunds, L. (1975) *Chance and Intelligence in Thucydides*, Cambridge MA: Harvard University Press.
Finley Jr, J.H. (1942) *Thucydides*, Cambridge MA: Harvard University Press.
Gomme, A.W. (1937) "The Greatest War in Greek History," in *Essays in Greek History and Literature* 116–124, Oxford: Basil Blackwell.
Hunter, V.J. (1973) *Thucydides, the Artful Reporter*, Toronto: Toronto University Press.
Rawlings III, H.R. (1981) *The Structure of Thucydides' History*, Princeton: Princeton University Press.
Romilly, J. de (1963) *Thucydides and Athenian Imperialism*, transl. P. Thody, Oxford: Oxford University Press.

XENOPHON

Anderson, J.K. (1974) *Xenophon*, London: Duckworth.
Dillery, J. (1995) *Xenophon and the History of his Times*, London and New York: Routledge.

FRAGMENTARY HISTORIANS

Barber, G.L. (1935) *The Historian Ephorus*, Cambridge: Cambridge University Press.
Brown, T.S. (1958) *Timaeus of Tauromenium*, Berkeley: University of California Press.
Brunt, P.A. (1980) "On Historical Fragments and Epitomes," *Classical Quarterly* 30: 477–494.
Connor, W.R. (1967) "History without Heroes: Theopompus' Treatment of Philip of Macedon," in *Greek, Roman and Byzantine Studies* 8: 133–154.
Flower, M.A. (1994) *Theopompus of Chios: History and Rhetoric in the Fourth Century B.C.*, Oxford: Clarendon Press.
Pearson, L. (1960) *The Lost Histories of Alexander the Great*, London: American Philological Association.
—— (1987) *The Greek Historians of the West: Timaeus and his Predecessors*, Atlanta: American Philological Association.

POLYBIUS

Sacks, K. (1981) "Polybius on the Writing of History", *Classical Studies*, University of California Publications, vol. 24, Berkeley and Los Angeles: University of California Press.

Walbank, F.W. (1972) *Polybius*, Berkeley and Los Angeles: University of California Press.

INDEX

149